Understand Your New Life In Christ

I'M SAVED! NOW WHAT?

Mark 11:22-25
You can move
mountains ♥

JAMIE BARRERA

Jamie Barrera

DALLAS, TEXAS

Higgins Publishing | www.higginspublishing.com - The publisher is not responsible for websites (or their content) that are not owned by the publisher. Higgins Publishing is committed to excellence in the publishing industry. The company reflects the philosophy established by the founder, based on Psalm 68:11, 'The Lord gave the word, and great was the company of those who published it.'

Library of Congress Control Number: 2022904099 May 2022

pcm 282 – Includes Index

Barrera, Jamie – I'm Saved! Now What? *Understand Your New Life in Christ*

Higgins Publishing 2nd Edition

English: 978-1-941580-94-3 (PB) * 978-1-941580-56-1(HB) * 978-1-941580-95-0 (EB)
978-1-941580-88-2 (AB) Audio Book

Spanish: 978-1-941580-89-9 (PB) * 978-1-941580-26-4 (EB

REL012000 RELIGION / Christian Living / General
REL011000 RELIGION / Christian Education / General
REL012120 RELIGION / Christian Living / Spiritual Growth

Please post a review at
HigginsPublishing.com or at Amazon
to let Jamie, know that you enjoyed this book.

Sign up for Jamie's newsletter for giveaways, encouragement and free content at JamieJBarrera.com.

~~~

Request prayer, volunteer for outreach, donate, or schedule Jamie for speaking engagements and virtual tours at, JamieJBarrera.com.

Please share Jamie's posts and podcasts at her website to help others with their Christian journey.

Thank you!

A percentage of the proceeds from sales of "I'm Saved! Now What?" are donated to Jamie's non-profit organization at JamieJBarrera.com.

I'm Saved! Now What?
Is also available in the following formats:
Audiobook & Ebook in English,
Paperback & Ebook in Spanish.
~~~

Romans 8:28 New International Version (NIV)

And we know that in all things God works for the good of those who love him, who have been called according to his purpose.

DEDICATION

This gift is for edification of the church. (1 Corinthians 14:12). For every new believer who is entering into God's will for their life.

For every believer who desires to step back into God's will, God has never left you or forsaken you. Our Father's will and purpose for everyone is an investment that will take us from our current places, no matter what they look like, into new beginnings.

With the humblest gratitude, love, and honor of the late prophet, pastor, teacher, mighty anointed man of God: Dr. Danny DiAngelo, founder of Genesis Worship Center, and his family, who faithfully and beautifully poured their hearts into the impartation of theological seeds of knowledge, the meaning of being a worshiper and kingdom faith into the GWC family, around the world, including me and my daughter. We faithfully served under his covering with earnest devotion for twelve years until his passing.

We love and miss you deeply.

ACKNOWLEDGMENTS

My Father, Lord, my Savior: for drawing me into Your presence and adopting me as Your daughter. Thank You for Your provision, sustaining me, and Your protection. Thank You, God, for trusting, equipping, and anointing me with this book for You. Your love is great and everlasting. You are Mighty!

Those who, in every season of my life, took the time to invest the Word of God in my soul. The ones who saw greatness when I saw the opposite. Those who called to see if I was okay during my trials and tests. My living ministering angels, whom God sent to keep me going. I thank you greatly. My Grams, Maria. The most beautiful angel I know in life and in heaven.

My daughter, Celina Maria. My miracle who changed my life. Every day, you teach me the meaning of love. Deliverance and life worth living came because God blessed me with you. I love you BIGGER than the giants! You are my everything and the answer to my prayers. You are the BEST thing that has ever happened to me. I love you; I love you; I love you!

TABLE OF CONTENTS

FOREWORD

Jamie is what I call a "fireball" for Jesus Christ. She is a dedicated believer who desires to see others grow to their fullest potential. In her new book, *"I'm Saved! Now What?"*, Jamie tackles the greatest challenges of what to do after you receive the gift of salvation as well as how to apply God's Word to your everyday life. This is more than just a great book to read, it is a spiritual guide and handbook that you can study to learn valuable truths.

What I love about Jamie's writings is her passion and ability to be used as a vessel to catapult you from where you are now into your God-given purpose and destiny in life. You will grow and you will know what your next destiny step is by going on this incredible journey with her. I highly recommend this book for all ages and backgrounds.

Debra George
Debra George Ministries
Stafford, Texas

INTRODUCTION

There has always been a hunger for God within me. There was so much knowledge that I sought to know, but I didn't know Him, nor where to begin to find the answers to many questions. My soul's desire became a curiosity to seek meaning, then, to find out who is God. Through the years, the more I knew of the Lord, the more my determination grew. God showed me who He is through trial and error experiencing the lessons the hard way, observing, and building a relationship with God. Those lessons opened my mind to understanding the ways of my Father. As I lived out every season of my life, recognizing that it was God's hand teaching and testing me, not bad luck. My Father (God) let me experience different situations that opened my eyes to understanding that changed my heart posture. It took years to accept the convictions of my heart and the willingness to submit to change. Much like Moses, I was never eloquent or articulate in speaking to people, but God gave me an outlet to say what He placed on my heart to say through writing. It's His thoughts, not mine. I am just the vehicle being used in a mighty way for His Kingdom through discovery in dark tough places.

I grew up in extreme hardship. Stability was difficult when I gave my heart to the Lord at 17. I was the first to accept Jesus but with no guidance and no foundation, naturally, I had tons of questions. Every question I had about God, either people did not know how to answer the questions and mask it with an "Oh, you're a baby Christian" answer, or the people whom I asked would look at me as if I should have known the answer all along. I stopped asking. By the time I hit 21, a series of heartbreaking life-changing events occurred, including the death of my grandmother who helped raise my sister and me. I hit a downward spiral for a five-year season of rebellion. At the birth of my daughter, everything changed. I made a promise to God that with or without help, I planned to keep that promise to stay holy and grounded in His way, His truth, and in His life for myself and the sake of my daughter. Even though I did not know where to begin, my eyes were opened to see God's hands in everything that unwaveringly led me to want more of Him in the pit of the dark places. With the help of the Holy Spirit, the process of ridding every toxic thing out of my life began, even in some repeated cycles that finally broke away from me.

I needed to know why I have gone through so much pain and hardship which led to my purpose. God opened the door to street ministry through my teacher, mentor, and spiritual mother, the mighty soul winner for Jesus, world-renowned evangelist Debra George. In those outreaches through her ministry all across the country, I met gang members, drug dealers, strippers, prostitutes, homeless, and single parents in tough impoverished neighborhoods who did not know Christ but wanted to know and needed Jesus for themselves and their families. The same pain and hardships I encountered for years in one way or another were the people to whom God led me to minister. In 2016, in the middle of a hard season of transformation, pruning, and transition, God prompted me to write this book for you.

The main questions from those who just accepted Christ were "I don't know what to do next... What does *that* (church reference) mean exactly? I don't know what you are talking about?" I had the same questions at 17; I'm sure you don't know or the person who just discovered Jesus doesn't know, either. It does not mean that we are stupid for not knowing the mysteries of God or His Kingdom or what *that* church word means. These questions are an understanding that we need Jesus in every area of our life. What has confused new believers is an overly complex conversion from Genesis to Revelation, especially for those who never grew up in church, have lived lives only through worldly views and concepts.

Although knowing the Bible from beginning to the end is extremely important. New believers need something more practical and simplified that leads them to the full picture and purpose of the Kingdom of God for them. I wrote down every question because as a new believer I did not know what to do next. Those are the questions of want and need for the Lord that you too might be searching for.

This book is to teach someone once they received Jesus into their heart and be a tool for discipleship for new believers. With each chapter, I hope this is the starting point of your journey and the discovery of personal reflections to help you develop the passion to go deeper in Christ Jesus. I promise this will not be overly complicated. I will try to keep it as simplified as possible. I pray your heart is willing to know God's Word for your life. I pray that your mind, heart, and soul are open with a stirring that burns within to the changes that are happening in your life. I ask that you don't close this book or the door on God when it gets hard or at the moment you do not understand situations or circumstances. Keep going, keep searching, keep knocking. God will meet you in that place that you are longing for. Don't let anyone stop you. You have to see what God has in store for you. You have to see the new talents that God will show you. You have to keep going for the blessings and gifts God wants to give you at each level as you grow.

There is so much more than today. It's a journey. It's your story full of deliverance, healing, liberty with signs, wonders, and miracles that follow. This is your first step; the door is open to a deep relationship that is forever. Welcome to the Kingdom of God. I pray that the oil of gladness fills you into overflowing every single step of the way.

Romans 12:2 (NIV)

Do not conform to the pattern of this world, but be transformed by the renewing of your mind. Then you will be able to test and approve what God's will is—his good, pleasing and perfect will.

CHAPTER 1
CONFESSION / REPENT

Matthew 4:17 (NIV)

From that time on Jesus began to preach,
"Repent, for the kingdom of heaven has come near."

First thing to understand is that with God there is always a process and order. In the Gospels, when Jesus encountered people, Jesus addressed the sin and their faith to believe that He is the Son of God before the healings deliverance and miracles had taken place. Let's ask ourselves a few personal questions before we go into the rest of this book. Are you sure you are going to heaven? Did you or did you not decide to want to know Christ as your personal Lord and Savior? Are you at a point in your life where there is no other way but God's way? Jesus says, "*For God so loved the world, that he gave his only Son, that whoever believes in him should not perish but have eternal life*" (John 3:16). Jesus being your Lord and Savior is not about a denomination; God wants a relationship with you now and eternally just the way you are right at this moment. God is not looking for perfect people; God wants the broken people to turn them into a magnet for miracles. God loves you; God knows you, and God sees your need. This call is to offer God to reign over your life and to know what the Kingdom of Heaven is like on earth and eternally. God wants to use you for His glory, to be a shining light in dark places. God wants to make you influential, change the atmosphere and multiply to prosper. God wants to use your past and turn it into a very blessed testimony with a Kingdom purpose to bless others, because your faith to believe that Jesus is the Son of God has made you well. Maybe you are coming back from being distant from God in a moment when you lost your way or gave up hope. That term is *backsliding*. However, new journeys can always start today. If you are not sure you are going to heaven, and are willing to position your heart, mind, soul, and spirit to see and believe in a transformation that only God can do, I would like to pray a quick prayer with you before we begin.

> *Father, I come to you in the name of Jesus. I know I lived a life that has separated me from You. I ask for Your forgiveness for missing the mark that led me into sin. I accept Jesus into my heart, and I believe You died for my sins and rose from the dead so I can have eternal life with You. I receive, trust, and follow You as my Lord, Savior, and guide over my life. Help me to do Your will and redeem my soul. In Jesus's name, Amen.*

Alright! You did it! You just asked God to save you from rebellion, which is the sin that leads to death not just physically but spiritually as well. I am so proud of you! That is a brave step you just took. It's a personal step and an emotional step.

I'm saved! Now, what?

Either you felt something, or you didn't, but something happened you just don't know what, right? *Faith* is confidence in what we hope for and the assurance that the Lord is working on our behalf, even though we cannot see it. For some people, there is an immediate change. For others the change is gradual; 'time' is your friend, but faith in God is the assurance we have that God is healing, restoring what is out of order. It depends on the person and how God is teaching you regarding His plan to use you for His purpose which is the reason why you were born. God might need to heal or break some things to get you back into alignment with Him. This is your individual journey. Your walk will be completely different from everybody else's; nobody has it all together. Once you are saved, you are saved eternally; it is the Holy Spirit who does a good work in you to fulfill His purpose (Philippians 2:13). I have heard people say, "*Is that person really saved?*" What they are asking is, "Is that person **fully transformed** in Christ?" Your journey is a transformation process. This is a relationship that needs to be built. With relationships we must keep building it up, connecting, and getting to know one another. Mistakes happen; we are human. We fall, but we get back up. Sometimes people accept Jesus and are in the worst situations; it takes time to evolve out of habitats and environments. Saved? What does that mean? If you are still not sure what *salvation* is, I am happy to share it with you.

Salvation

> Source of being saved or delivered, taken out of a place from harm, ruin, or loss.

Salvation: God saved your soul from a life that leads to death or destruction in this life and eternally. There is a heaven and a hell, but we have a choice to choose where we will end up when we die. Many fear their eternal life. Many do not understand the reality of heaven and hell. Everyone who dies does not automatically go to heaven. Heaven is not a hallucinated cartoon state of nirvana. The devil is not a little red person on your shoulder. Hell is not a party surrounded by fire, drugs, sex, and rock and roll.

What is heaven and hell like?

Heaven is described as eternal comfort: Revelation 21:4 "He will wipe every tear from their eyes. There will be no more death 'or mourning or crying or pain, for the old order of things has passed away."

Hell is described as eternal torment: Revelation 21:8 "the cowardly, the unbelieving, the vile, the murderers, the sexually immoral, those who practice magic arts, the idolaters and all liars—they will be consigned to the fiery lake of burning sulfur."

When you die your soul goes into one of these two places. How does someone know they are going to heaven? People say "*I've been a good person… I donate to the poor… I love everybody…My life is good…*" We live in a world under the control of the devil, but God has all authority. All wrongdoing is sin, and there are sins that do not lead to a physical death, but there are sins that do lead to death (1 John 5:17). When you follow the ways of the world you might not think sin is wrong because it satisfies a desire. Some people live in such dysfunction and chaos, their environment has become their normal. When you accept Jesus into your heart, the devil must go to the courts in heaven to ask permission to attack you (Job 2). You are under God's protection. The Bible says that it is by grace you have been saved from the eternal torment which is a place of weeping and gashing of teeth (Matthew 24:51). Jesus says there is only one way to heaven. Jesus is the way and the truth and the life. No one comes to the Father in Heaven except through Jesus (John 14:6). By faith we declare with our mouth, "Jesus is Lord," *(Lord has dominion, rule, reign, authority)* and believe in our hearts that God raised Jesus from the dead, we will be saved.

1 John 5:13-14a

I write these things to you who believe in the name of the Son of God so that you may know that you have eternal life. This is the confidence we have in approaching God

When you are declaring for yourself that "Jesus is Lord," what you are admitting is that Jesus has full control or dominion (dominance) over your life. Transformation is happening that shifts from our plans to God's plans, giving God the authority to help change our ways and heal our bodies. For example, growing up, I wanted to be a dancer in a Broadway theater, but God called me to minister to women who are in strip clubs in San Francisco on the street called Broadway. After a few broken feet accidents, I realized that dancing was not the plan God had for me, and God had to help me discover the rest. I knew the life of a dancer; I knew the nightclub lifestyle from working in nightclubs in my early 20's. I was so excited to find a harvest and access to these ladies to speak the goodness of Jesus into their lives. God gave me a plan of saving souls through a world that most people find provocative. Then, He showed me another path of multiplication of souls either physically speaking the Word of God or through writing a book. That was my call, and I accepted it because God is always moving. God will present opportunities to you. It is your choice to accept or deny those calls, yet sometimes we miss the mark because we did not recognize blessings that was presented before us because it originally did not look or feel like something that could be a good thing. God must reveal the hidden things in its proper time. Before my path was revealed to me, I had to completely change my surroundings and get things in order to make room for God's call. It is funny how God works that way. Transformation started with the convictions that were placed on my heart by the Holy Spirit.

Confession

Acknowledgment or to disclose, profess, admission (**admitting**).

Repentance

Awareness of your sin (rebellion) that convicts/prompts you to turn away (**change your mind/change direction**) from an action or habit.

Remorse

Deep and painful regret for wrongdoing.

For most people, confession is the first step. What does that mean? If you grew up Catholic as I did, we always heard "confess your sins." To be honest, most people didn't really know the extent of the significance of the meaning of confession to repentance. It was beyond stealing candy from a jar, praying a prayer of "I am sorry" and you're fine. There was an understanding that one had to admit their wrongdoings, but I was never instructed about turning away from actions until later in life. When God convicts our hearts of our behaviors, remorse is a command to change our perspective of the situation of our actions. The moment we accepted Jesus as our Lord and Savior we were set free from condemnation *(punishment; sentencing)* (Romans 8:1) that sin brings. God will point out the areas He wants us to let go of and change for our good. The change God requires of one person will be different for another. Understand sin is sin, no matter how big or small, no matter the sin God wants the sin out of our life. The area of our individual change is always tied to our purpose that God planned for our life. Confession is NOT a prayer of remorse to say I am sorry. Jesus did not command remorse. Jesus commanded repentance. Repentance is a command for change in our thoughts and in the direction of our actions.

Confession is the starting tool on how to let go of the toxic behaviors mentally, physically, and emotionally that were hindering one's life. There are two parts to confession; both have to do with the words of your mouth. The first part of confession is **not** remorse. Confession does not mean "I am sorry." Confession is admitting that "Yes I did x, y, or z." Sometimes, we have to confess our part or why we chose to react toward the sin or temptations instead of choosing another outcome. Confession is freely admitting our reaction in each situation. It is helping us to look at our heart posture in our actions instead of blaming other people. "They did this to me." No, we played a role too. "They" might have done a, b, or c but our reaction was x, y, or z. Here is where repentance comes in. First, admit our reaction and our part to the situation. I confess my part of x, y, or z, not "I am sorry," but legitimately taking responsibility for our actions. Remorse is the feeling that tells us our actions were wrong. Emotions are natural to help us comprehend or feel our situation. Confession is admission; it is an act of recognition. Two different things. God does not want us to stop there. God wants us to change our perspective of thinking so that next time we react in a completely different way. When we repent, we are making a deliberate choice to change our minds about doing certain things asking ourselves where did we step over the boundaries that have caused a conflict of any kind. We are telling God, "I do not want to do x, y, or z or react a certain way ever again." Then confess our desire to know and want what God wants in our lives, and to respond the way God would respond. Repentance is a personal decision to change our minds and behavioral habits with remorse for actions that are unhealthy and dysfunctional. The main instruction is not a confession; the main command is to repent. To change our minds and change our direction. God wants our actions to align with His actions. Remorse helps reveal our fleshly nature that is against a Christ-like nature. Confession helps us to admit that we need to change our minds or perception regarding our actions.

Confession, which in this case, is the Hebrew word *yadah*, which means "to cast out;" the stem verb is confessing sins. Remove yourself from or "cast out" bad habits. The second part of confession is the Greek word *homologeō*, which means "to say the same thing as another," the stem verb is "to agree with." We confess with our words and agree that Jesus is the Son of God. Confess that Jesus is Lord over our lives. When it comes to salvation, our confession is to magnify Jesus in our lives, not our sin. The confession *homologeō* is our word declaration and agreement of truth. *Yadah* is the tool toward repentance, casting out the bad to declare the good.

Romans 10:9-10 (NIV)

If you declare with your mouth, "Jesus is Lord," and believe in your heart that God raised him from the dead, you will be saved. For it is with your heart that you believe and are justified, and it is with your mouth that you profess your faith and are saved.

Walking out our salvation is supposed to be tough and uncomfortable because it is stripping us of our carnality into whom we are supposed to be in the Kingdom of God. Jesus says those who enter into the Kingdom of Heaven have to go through the narrow gate (Matthew 7:13). He is saying you are not going to enter by foolishness or wickedness but in separation from a worldly view. Our effort is not common but a holy and pure life in public and in private, allowing the Holy Spirit to fully transform our hearts to change to God's way. The way to life is so narrow that it may easily be missed, it is about true discipline. It must be sought after and only a few find it; meaning you must make a deliberated decisional effort to do what is right in God's eyes. We stand on the Word of God even if it makes us unpopular and opposes what everyone else is doing. My hope that when you read this chapter, you will understand the importance and difference between confession and repentance.

Romans 12:2a (NLT)

"Don't copy the behavior and customs of this world, but let God transform you into a new person by changing the way you think."

Jesus died on the cross for our sins. The first demand Jesus made was to repent. In the Gospel of Matthew, after Jesus performed his first miracle of water into wine, He spent 40 days alone in the wilderness being tempted by the devil. After Jesus came out from the 40 days of wilderness the first words that He preached were located in Matthew 4:17.

Matthew 4:17 New International Version (NIV)

From that time on Jesus began to preach,
"Repent, for the kingdom of heaven has come near."

A brief overview of sin. In Genesis 3 of the Bible, after Eve ate the *forbidden fruit*, both Adam and Eve hid from God. God gave them both a series of questions that were open opportunities to confess and repent for disobeying God's instruction. Instead of confessing and repenting, they started to blame each other for their sin. Adam, Eve, and the serpent had to suffer the consequences for their actions.

Habit

1. an acquired behavior pattern regularly followed until it has become almost involuntary:
2. a particular practice, custom, or usage
3. a dominant or regular disposition or tendency; prevailing character or quality: bodily or physical condition
4. addiction, especially to narcotics (often preceded by the): mental character or disposition

It is definitely okay to reassess yourself. Some behaviors do not look bad on the surface but too much of a good thing can become toxic or vice versa. Some behaviors might start off bad in someone's perspective, but the end result is good.

Example #1

You got Facebook to connect with friends and family. However, you never intended to stay online that much. You saw your friends and family's lives posted in stories and pictures on the news feed. Now you are constantly sharing your stories and pictures. Now you are on Facebook at work, not working. You are on Facebook at home and ignoring your family. On vacation, you cannot have a good vacation without the best vacation selfie. Your Facebook habit turned into an addiction and time wasted.

Example #2

Your health issues have required you to change your diet. You do not like "healthy" food. Instead of the usual doughnut or pancakes you opt for egg whites and Greek yogurt. Instead of pizza every Friday night you started eating baked chicken and asparagus. After two months of giving up processed fast food you no longer choose unhealthy food. Your taste buds have changed and now your body is used to healthy food choices. You're eating habits now contributed to a healthier lifestyle of eating right and exercise. You feel good and you look good.

Look at your life and ask yourself, being honest, "What do you think is normal?" Research areas of improvement that you know you can do better. Start small and balance; less of one thing for more of another. Start your morning off with a quick prayer before you get out of bed. Drink tea instead of coffee. These are little changes. Then ask in prayer "Lord help me to stop smoking or gossiping..." Whatever it is that is affecting you to function in the best that you can be physically, mentally, and emotionally; recognize, confess, and repent. Ask yourself, "Is this habit now a part of my character? How is it affecting the world around me?" Ask the Holy Spirit to help you change.

Romans 10:17 (ESV)

"So faith comes from hearing, and hearing through the word of Christ."

There are things in our life that we feel or know immediately that we are doing or have done that come to our mind right now that are wrong. It might be a big conviction or a little conviction, but our hearts are being convicted, nonetheless. I want you to know that it is a great thing to have the convictions of our hearts. It doesn't feel good, but it is the start of a transformation. Do not ever ignore your intuition. Awareness and acknowledgment are supposed to happen. Those convictions of our hearts are the areas in our lives that God wants to work on with us so we can recognize that "area" to repent of whatever "it" is in order for us to have better lives in Him. These areas of "iniquity" (rebellion) are the areas we must submit to God.

When I first came to Christ, I didn't know Jesus well enough to have a real relationship with Him. However, there was something that I heard that lead me to want to begin this journey. It was within the convictions of my heart that I said, "there has to be a better way." I wanted the Holy Spirit, Jesus, and God that I saw in people. I wanted that in me, not the deep dirty places that I lived with all my life. The moment one hears God's voice pulling our hearts to come to the altar to accept Jesus Christ as our Savior, an understanding accrued that Jesus is trying to save us and cleanse us from the life we were living into the purpose of God. This is the moment of opportunity for you to make a choice of stepping into God's will and plan for your life, repent or perish (Luke 13:1-5). It is your choice to follow the pulling of your heart knowing that it is a gentle tug and pull of the Holy Spirit within ourselves calling us into this moment to tell our soul there is a better way. The 'call' of God is a divine summons for a vocation of divine impartation of a Kingdom assignment or position for the purpose of His glory. To magnify God here on earth, by repentance we put our own sin and self-interest to death in exchange for a new life in Christ, to be 'born again'.

Hebrews 11:1 (AMP)

"Now faith is the assurance (substance, title deed, confirmation) of things hoped for (divinely guaranteed), and the evidence of things not seen [the conviction of their reality—faith comprehends as fact what cannot be experienced by the physical senses]."

Faith=Seed | Prayer=Planted | Change=Growth

I Corinthians 3:5-9

What, after all, is Apollos? And what is Paul? Only servants, through whom you came to believe—as the Lord has assigned to each his task. ***I (Paul) planted the seed, Apollos watered it, but God has been making it grow.*** *So neither the one who plants nor the one who waters is anything, but only God, who makes things grow. The one who plants and the one who waters have one purpose, and they will each be rewarded according to their own labor. For we are co-workers in God's service; you are God's field, God's building.*

Throughout the Bible, God uses planting and harvesting as an analogy, which is a comparison between two things to something else in significant respects, typically for the purpose of explanation or clarification. For example, planting a seed and watching it grow. In the next chapter, we will talk more about sin pertaining to the "fruit" and the "root." When you pray, ask what God wants for you. God hears those prayers; the prayer becomes a planted seed that will yield a harvest. God will honor what you ask of Him according to His purpose, not our agenda. When you pray, that is your faith *(believing that God is, can and will do)* no matter how big or small or what your situation looks like currently because nothing is impossible for God. When we pray for change, change will come. When you repent, you change your mind concerning the things that have been toxic in your life. Your willingness to let go and let God is when those seeds start to grow. The Holy Spirit within you helps reveal the toxic things that need to be removed out of your life. It is your choice to let those toxic things go and to make room for the good to come.

1 Samuel 16:7 (ESV)

But the Lord said to Samuel, "Do not look on his appearance or on the height of his stature, because I have rejected him. For the Lord sees ***not as man sees:*** *man looks on the outward appearance, but* ***the Lord looks on the heart.****"*

You prayed a prayer; therefore, you believed that something would happen. You changed; therefore, you grew into the direction of God's goodness for your life. Then, you wake up one day and realize, "I am not the same anymore." The anxiety is gone, and you are healed emotionally, mentally, spiritually, even physically. Transformation takes time. Do not ever question your prayer. Your prayer is a seed, and God heard your prayer. God always looks at your heart. You prayed, that means you believe no matter how big or small your faith is. God saw your faith in action, and God heard your prayer. God assessed your request and actions that came from your heart. The next step is making the changes and room in your heart, mind, soul, and spirit. This includes even making room in your surroundings and associations for God's transformation to take its rightful place for a good purpose. Part of the discovery of God's love for you is to build a relationship with God. God works in you so that you can grow in the way He had intended you to be when He chose and created you. Always remember "If you will, God will." You prayed, God answers. You made the changes, now God provides. You sowed (planted) the seed, now God supplies the need to bring you into a season of growth. Ask God to reveal the areas in your heart that needs change and ask God for daily repentance.

Father, in Jesus's name, convict my heart and reveal to me every area that You would like me to change. As I declare that You are Lord over my life, I grant You access to take full control in the journey of change. I confess of ________ and I repent (change my mind) of this. Forgive me Father of all things knowing and unknowing, willing and unwilling that did not align with Your heart, mind, and purpose. Make in me a clean heart with right motives and make in me a right sounding mind. Help me Holy Spirit to stay focused on Your will and not my own for the purpose of divine transformation for the Kingdom of God. I ask that my will be Your will, in the precious name of your Son Jesus's name, Amen.

CHAPTER 2
SIN - FRUIT & ROOT

Galatians 5:19-26 (NIV)

The acts of the flesh are obvious: sexual immorality, impurity, and debauchery; idolatry and witchcraft; hatred, discord, jealousy, fits of rage, selfish ambition, dissensions, factions, and envy; drunkenness, orgies, and the like. I warn you, as I did before, that those who live like this will not inherit the kingdom of God.

But the fruit of the Spirit is love, joy, peace, forbearance, kindness, goodness, faithfulness, gentleness, and self-control. Against such things, there is no law. Those who belong to Christ Jesus have crucified the flesh with its passions and desires. Since we live by the Spirit, let us keep in step with the Spirit. Let us not become conceited, provoking and envying each other.

As it was mentioned in chapter one, the Bible likes to use the analogy from a farmer's perspective. There are good fruit and bad fruit, good versus evil. Each fruit comes from a branch that has a root attached to it. Once a good healthy tree touches a little bit of poison, the poison spreads to try to completely kill not just the fruit but the branch and the root it came from. In order to change your character through repentance, the best way to change is to dig a little deeper to find the root source that is hidden underneath the surface of the problem. The root has a branch that comes above the surface that you see. The branch is where the fruit is that you eat. You have good fruit and rotten fruit. The source is in the root, so if the root isn't dealt with then the problem continues. We have to get to the root. An English preacher and teacher from the 1800's, Charles Spurgeon said, "*Almost saved is altogether lost.*" Another way to say it, we cannot just remove the cobweb, we have to kill the spider.

Matthew 7:16-18 (NIV)

By their fruit, you will recognize them. Do people pick grapes from thornbushes or figs from thistles? Likewise, every good tree bears good fruit, but a bad tree bears bad fruit. A good tree cannot bear bad fruit, and a bad tree cannot bear good fruit.

There is more to "sin" *(rebellion)* than meets the eye. The root of sin is division from God. There are deeper roots and connections in the sinful world that make temptations seem normal and society says "it's okay" to the natural flesh. **We are all sinners**. We were all born into sin with temptations to sin on every side that has caused us to slip off the right path. Sin appeals to the appetite of our desires, leaning toward a false satisfaction. There are angels to help us and there are demons to destroy our lives. That is why the devil tempts a person into doing/teaching the things they desire or feel like a certain action needs to happen in a perverted and distorted way that seems attractive or fun. Temptations *(a thing or course of action that attracts someone in a desirous fashion)* look like fun, good things, or good decisions so we can give in and say yes to the start of a downward spiral that is meant to destroy what God meant for good. Sin comes from our hearts (Matthew 15:19). Too much of a good thing can make one sick and lead to death. Sin is not only an action and choice, but it is an evil spirit of a liar ready to steal, kill, and destroy (John 10:10), in that order. Sin is the division between us, God, and our purpose. The bigger the attack on our lives, the bigger the purpose God has for us. When a sinner decides to stop being rebellious and repents in the faith that God has given them, they accept the ways of God, then their life and heart are changed forever in unity and love. God is love, but God also gets angry and corrects as a good Father corrects His children.

You and I, we were not perfect. God is perfect. God knows how to reach a person's heart. He loves us just where we are, but God has zero-tolerance for sin. As God gave us grace and mercy, we also give others grace and mercy, not judgement but compassion. If you have done something, please do not point out someone else's faults and pasts to cover your own issues you yourself do not want to face. If someone starts to argue with you about their sins, just know that they are not ready to receive the blood of Jesus which washes away and cleanses people of their sin. Our true identity is only going to be found in Christ through our hearts. Our job is to love, not bring up someone's past. God can use anyone's broken past for His glory.

Sin can be a powerful stronghold. All the medication, therapy, and money in the world cannot break sin. The **only thing more powerful** that can completely set someone free from sin is the Holy Spirit that will penetrate through the heart and blood of Jesus Christ that cleanses all manners of their perspective regarding the sin. It is through our hearts and a shift of our minds that there will be a full transformation. The fruit is the evidence of what has been planted into us either through people, environments, or the Holy Spirit. The fruit is our obvious behavior; it is evidence of who we are right now. It shows what kind of person we are becoming. As we talk about the good and the bad, remember you have a choice. God gives you the right to choose, but you are not free from the consequences of your choice. If you choose good it is a blessing, if you choose wrong it is destruction.

To understand sin, you have to understand spiritual warfare. The source of sin is mentioned in the beginning. The first book of the Bible is Genesis. In the 3rd chapter, the original sin is referenced or the "fall of man" in most Bibles. The focus of the chapter is for you to recognize the fruit and the root of sin and the revelation of God's character and likeness. It is important to understand the source from which all sin began. Understanding this story will give you a better picture of how a snake in the first book of the Bible becomes a dragon beast in the last book of Revelation. All it takes is one spark to become an inferno.

This is a quick overview of Adam and Eve. They lived happy, loving, and secure walking and talking with God directly in God's presence in the Garden of Eden, which means delight and pleasure. God created a place for them to live without any struggle and in communion with Him. Adam and Eve were able to indulge in everything they wanted. They could eat the multitude of fruits and vegetables from any plant provided, except one. There were two trees in the middle of the garden. The "Tree of Life" and the "Tree of the Knowledge of good and evil." The instruction was to not eat from the Tree of Knowledge, or they would die. Satan who is skilled in deception (a liar) (Gen. 3:1) showed his envious disposition in their living situation and their close covenant to the one and only Mighty God. Satan enters the garden as a serpent and used their loving trust against Eve with manipulation. He tells Eve that the fruit is in fact good to eat, and they will not actually die. Eve eats the fruit then gives it to Adam. With the power of the fruit, they both become aware of knowing good from evil. Adam and Eve are now aware they are naked and exposed in disobedience. They hide in fig tree leaves covering their nakedness. They hear God coming to commune with them in His presence as they do every day. They hide from God due to their shame. God in his loving kindness removed the shame leaves and clothed Adam and Eve in garments He made for them as well as giving each a consequence for their actions. This is the first example of the motive of the devil's assignment that is a predator seeking to devour.

1 Peter 5:8 Amplified Bible (AMP)

Be sober [well balanced and self-disciplined], be alert and cautious at all times. That enemy of yours, the devil, prowls around like a roaring lion [fiercely hungry], seeking someone to devour.

The devil also comes in to entice and tempt a person (1 Thessalonians 3:5, Matthew 4:3) with what is in their heart to covet. The tempters mission is to entice and test someone to do evil. What does it mean to covet? To desire or yearn for something that is not yours. God owns everything. This was the first principle of stewardship and honor. Which is the same principle in the financial tithe. God owned the land and the tree and the fruit. God said you can have anything you want except this tree and fruit of it. The tree of the Knowledge of good and evil belonged to God. Eve and Adam did not honor what belongs to God and stole the fruit that was God's property. When Adam and Eve broke their covenant with God, listening to the serpent they submitted to the devil, stealing and eating the fruit which at the time seemed harmless. In fact, it caused a rift between humanity and God that Jesus had to come to earth to bring humanity and God back together by shedding His blood on the cross of Calvary, breaking the natural and scientific laws of death by becoming alive again on the third day, walking and talking with His people for an additional forty days before taking His seat next to the Father in Heaven. That is how sin entered the earth. The devil came as a liar, a thief, a murderer, and destroyer of delightful and pleasurable (Eden) things and used Adam and Eve to accomplish his sinful plot on the earth.

James 1:15 Amplified Bible (AMP)

Then, after lust (illicit desire) has conceived, it gives birth to sin; and sin, when it is full-grown (run its course), gives birth to death.

This is what God meant when he said "you will certainly die" if you eat of the fruit. There are three traps according to 1 John 2:16.

1: Lust of the flesh
2: Lust of the eyes
3: Pride of life

Eve fell into all three in Genesis 3:5-6. She knew that if she ate the fruit, she would be like God knowing good from evil, she saw that the fruit was good to eat, and she desired that the fruit would make her wise. Now God enters the picture looking for Adam and Eve. They are hiding in their shame, covered in fig leaves. God asks them both giving them a chance to confess why they both know they are naked. Most people in their failures tend to blame others for their own faults. Adam blames the women and then he blames God because God gave her to him. Then the woman blames the serpent, and the serpent can't blame anyone because he was the mastermind behind the assault (Gen 3:11-13).

Now, the punishment; because everything has a cost. The serpent was cursed to crawl on the ground. The woman will bear children in pain. The man is cursed back into dust at death. We originally were not supposed to die, now there is death. Human labor that was once easy will now produce thorns and thistles making a man sweat for his work. Then the cherubim (angelic guardians of holy things and God) guard the Tree of Life and blocks the man from ever getting close to it. This is the preventative action from God so that no one can live forever in their sinful actions. However, Genesis 3:15 declares the first prophecy that Satan will be defeated.

Let's quickly jump to the last book of the Bible, Revelation. Revelation 20:2 introduces a giant "dragon, that ancient serpent, who is the devil, or Satan, and bound him for a thousand years." God has said in Genesis 3:15 that "open hostility between you (serpent) and the woman, and between your (woman) seed offspring (Jesus)." So, the serpent has grown to a dragon raging war against the seed of the woman.

Revelation 12:17

And the dragon was wroth (wrath/rage) with the woman (church), and went to make war with the remnant of her seed (believers), which keep the commandments of God, and have the testimony of Jesus Christ.

Genesis 3 is the starting point to get us back to the Gospel of Christ which we are instructed to go out into the world and share that God sacrificed His son for our sins. This makes us his remnant *(small remaining chosen people)* when we receive Jesus, we accept that we are children of God. Revelation says those children kept the commandments, which is the law. Jesus took on sin, bondages, curses, and sickness of the whole world at His death and rose again to set us free from the bondage of sin because of His shed blood. It is the righteousness and love of God and the sacrifice of Jesus that is more powerful than the torment and harassment of the devil. We call on the blood of Jesus because it was with His blood that we were saved from the damnation of hell.

Exodus 20 and Deuteronomy 5 tell the story of how Moses led the Israelites out of captivity and into the promised land. There God gives Moses the Ten Commandments listed on tablets for the chosen people of God to not live-in sin.

The 10 Commandments List:

1. You shall have no other gods before Me
   - ***(God is #1,** there is only one God)*
2. You shall **not** make idols
   - *(worship something or someone other than God as your top priority)*

3. You shall **not** take the name of the LORD your God in vain.
    - *(using His name to commit evil)*
4. Remember the Sabbath day (7th day), to **keep it holy.**
    - *(Day set apart for God; rest as God rested, reflect on His word)*
5. **Honor** your father and your mother.
    - *(Respect and hold to a high standard, that includes your spiritual parents)*
6. You shall **not** murder
    - *(homicide ether physical or of the heart)*
7. You shall **not** commit adultery
    - *(any sexual relations and thoughts w/ someone who is not your spouse)*
8. You shall **not** steal
    - *(take things that are not yours secretly, openly, fraudulently)*
9. You shall **not** bear false witness against any person.
    - *(lie and manipulated truth, deception)*
10. You shall **not** covet.
    - *(selfish desire and attempt to acquire a home, spouse, job, belongings that are not yours)*

Here is the list of the law. Actually, there are around 613 laws in the Old Testament which is in the Pentateuch *(first five books of the Bible)* known as the Torah (*Law*). These Ten Commandments are the instructions that God has held his people accountable to follow regarding their morality. The problem is **ALL** people fall into their sin (Romans 3:23). The other laws became more political. Throughout the Old Testament, the chosen people of God, the Israelites, would sacrifice an animal, the requirement is their best without blemish or deformity to signify purity, to shed its blood for their sins as an offering to the Lord for atonement (*making of amends for a wrong one has done*). Only the priest would take these sacrifices to the altar of God to atone for a sin committed over and over. That is why Jesus is our Lamb sacrifice of God that has taken away the sins of the world. An animal no longer is our atonement for sin; Jesus was our sin offering for our reparation. We share the testimony of Jesus who died on the cross and rose from the dead, revealing His divinity overpowering sin, which is and leads to death. Let's just rest assured that Jesus defeated death, hell, and the grave by dying on the cross, rising from the dead and ascending into heaven, giving us the Holy Spirit that lives within us to commune with God again as it was supposed to be before sin entered into the earth in Genesis chapter 3.

Seven Deadly Sins

Proverbs 6:16-19 Amplified Bible (AMP)

These six things the Lord ***hates;***
Indeed, seven are ***repulsive*** *to Him:*

A proud look [the attitude that makes one overestimate oneself and discount others], a lying tongue,

And hands that shed innocent blood (murders),
A heart that creates wicked plans,
Feet that run swiftly to evil,

A false witness who breathes out lies [even half-truths],
And one who spreads discord (rumors) among brothers.

In the beginning of Proverbs 6, God reminds us of our laziness and comfort in our lack, then proceeds to remind us of grotesque behaviors putting a command to change our ways otherwise our disaster shall come "without warning, and without relief" (Proverbs 6:15). Everything that God detests is what causes division; that is deceitful qualities of man He describes as wicked that makes sin the object to God's divine hatred. The things that God hates are the same things we must hate within ourselves. We could not be proud of our actions that are not harmonious in our lives that do not align with God's will. God says do not participate in "*sexual immorality, impurity, and debauchery; idolatry and witchcraft; hatred, discord, jealousy, fits of rage, selfish ambition, dissensions, factions, and envy; drunkenness, orgies, and the like*" (Galatians 5:19-26). There is no sin greater than the other, sin is sin. Rebellion speaks for itself. Any of these things we put in our lives as a priority over God, the Kingdom of God, our service to God is an idol. The consequences of sin are different. When a global illness hit in the beginning of 2020, all the idols of the world (Disney, MLB, NBA, NHL, UCL Soccer, Power 5 NCAA Conferences, Championships, work, schools, cities, nations, travel) had all shut down, but not churches. Then a National Day of Prayer was called. Why? It was a sign of God's improvement in the condition of this world. Then there was an attack on the church to shut it down. These events were preparations for revival, restoration of the church to a vital and fervent relationship with God after a period of moral decline. Rebellion leads to premature death. Death of relationships, death of purity, death of the body, death of trust, death to finances, death of generations. Sin does lead to death; this is the inward corrupt principles that we as humans give into.

Listed below are impure characteristics that God considers a sin that will lead to death. There is also a list of the opposing characteristics given to you by the Holy Spirit. You have a choice to choose one or the other, life or death, good or evil.

SIN Evil SPIRIT	Definition	Example	VIRTUE HOLY SPIRIT
Pride	A high or inordinate opinion of one's own dignity, importance, merit, superiority or position	Arrogance, conceit, vanity, self-centered, selfish ambition, attention seeking, rebellion, witchcraft, faction	Humility, meekness, love God, love others, love, appropriate acknowledgement of who you are. Selflessness
Envy	A feeling of discontent or covetousness with regard to another's advantages, success, possessions, etc.	Jealousy, covetousness, rivalry, discord, gossip, criticism with the intent to bring someone down, dissension	Love, joy, thankfulness, compassion, satisfaction, edification, gracious, encouragement, unity, discretion
Wrath	A strong, stern, or fierce anger; deeply resentful indignation	Anger, abuse, vengeful, fits of rage, hate, gossip, murder, division, hatred, cursing, foul mouth, witchcraft, rejection	Peace, gentleness, self-control, Joy, blessings, unity
Gluttony	Overindulgence, excessive indulgence	Addictions (drugs, alcohol), obesity, hoarder, idolatry, obsession, divination, debauchery	Self-control, contentment, patience, discernment, discipline, composure, discretion
Lust	Uncontrolled, intense or illicit sexual desire or appetite, craving, lasciviousness	Adultery, debauchery, homosexuality, bestiality, rape, orgies, porn, pedophilia, sexual immortality, false love of something or someone	Love, unselfishness, faithfulness, gentleness, unity, friendship, family, patience
Sloth	Disinclination to action or labor, spiritual apathy and inactivity	Laziness, procrastination, avoidance of work	Perseverance, diligence, servanthood, endurance, tenacity
Greed	A selfish and excessive/rapacious desire, especially for wealth or possessions.	Love of money / wealth / possessions, hungry for more never have enough,	Generosity, kindness, gratitude, bless others by giving, tithing

		bribery, thief, gambling	

Perverted: (of a thing) having been corrupted or distorted from its original course, meaning, or state.

> *Most commonly used* of a person or their actions characterized by sexually abnormal and unacceptable practices or tendencies.

When we become a child of God, we start to become unhappy in our sin. What was once entertaining become a foul taste in our mouths. Any participation makes us feel a sense of wrong, becoming miserable to be around those who love to live in their sins. I hear many people say, "I am free in Christ," which makes them think they have a pass to get drunk, gossip, be involved in one of the things that were listed above. The Bible says to live as free people, but do not use your freedom as a cover-up for evil (1 Peter 2:16). You cannot serve two masters (Matthew 6:24). God called you to be separate from the world to be an example and reflection of Him and His holiness (Romans 12:2, Ephesians 4:24). You are a representative of God's Kingdom (2 Corinthians 5:20). We must lose our plans in order to gain the fullness of Christ's plans for us (Matthew 10:39, 16:35). We cannot operate in selfish ambition and operate as a child of God at the same time or else be double-minded, which the Bible says a double-minded person is an unstable person in all of their ways (James 1:8).

The Bible says there are also pretenders, false believers. If you receive the truth and refuse to walk in the truth of God, you are denying God and His Word. Believers try to gently help people not walk in hypocrisy (Galatians 6:1). If the help is denied, their tendencies are those of a backslider or they were never a child of God, to begin with. Ask yourself this question, does anyone know you are a believer in Christ? God says you will know my people by their fruit (by their conduct) (Matthew 17:15-20). Do you obey the commands of Christ? I'm not asking if you are perfect. I'm asking if God says to walk in His way, will you do it? Not obey the commands you like and ignore the rest, but all of what God expects you to do? Sometimes we have to make a decision to avoid certain people and places that will allow the devil the opportunity to temp us. If you have a drinking problem, do not go to the bar or club and stay away from people who hang out there. Put yourself in a position to be around places and people who will build you up spiritually to help you love God and love people.

The devil will always pervert what God intended for unity, goodness, and purity. Everything the devil does is a counterfeit and distorted version of what God is trying to do in our lives. For example, when God brings in prosperity, the devil will bring poverty. There are evil spirits and there is the Holy Spirit. Where the Holy Spirit is, there is always love and unity, because God is love and a covenant God, meaning unbinding mutually beneficial relationships. The works of the devil are acts of lies in deception (John 8:44) that are set in order to steal, kill, and destroy us (John 10:10). His goal is to eliminate our existence completely. Where there is an evil spirit, we will always see deception and division in areas God wants us to prosper and give us a life of abundance.

Always remember the devil, his demons, principalities, evil forces, and powers of the kingdom of darkness (Ephesians 6:12) are well trained in the Word of God. Lucifer (*morning star son of the dawn*; Isaiah 14:12) was one of the covering cherubim in the angelic realm. He was the most beautiful and talented, who became arrogant in beauty, intelligence, power, and position that got him cast out of heaven (Ezekiel 28:12-18, Isaiah 14:12-17). He was persuasive enough to convince one-third of the angels to join him in his rebellion (Revelation 12:4).

Over thousands of years, he has crafted every single lie and temptation possible. He has studied us since birth and knows the call on our lives, our behaviors, and our desires. When assessing your life, look for the root, the things our parents exposed us to as children. The things since birth are where some of these sins started. The devil does not want us to complete God's purpose for our life. The devil does not want to see us succeed and will do everything in his power to stop us. God has a plan for you. God is all-knowing, more powerful, and has full dominion over any enemy. God is the one who created us with a plan and a purpose that gives us an abundantly prosperous life (Jeremiah 29:11).

Sin becomes idolatry in our life. Idolatry is excessive or blind adoration, reverence, and devotion to something or someone that is not God. It is also an image or other material object representing a deity to which religious worship is addressed that becomes witchcraft and divination. Where is our time, effort, and attention? Is it to the club or yoga? Are our name brand shoes or brand name electronic collection our obsession and objects of our affection? Or is the crush we are stalking on social media become our obsession? Have you found yourself codependent on something or someone to bring you satisfaction? Whatever is first in our life is our idol. That is who you worship. We might not think our number one "thing" is a religious thing, but it certainly has taken us away from other areas that are more important. The more we indulge in whatever has our time and attention, that becomes our character. List five things that are closest to you. That is your influence. If you hang around five intelligent people you will be the sixth. If you hang around five vulgar people you will become the sixth. It is the law of transfer and attraction. Who we surround ourselves with will reflects on our character. Do not be friends with wickedness. Let no corrupt thing come out of your mouth (Ephesians 4:29). We are either speaking blessings or cursing, there is no grey area. This is the image that we portray. Our behaviors and what we say are a reflection of our influences. What is your fruit?

Back then, the Israelites had to sacrifice animals for their sins. Jesus sacrificed Himself to pay for our sin offering. On the cross, Jesus took upon himself all forms of evil, curses, and punishment in exchange to give us a life that is prosperous and well taken care of. Sacrifices and offerings by blood were the customs to cleanse and bless. Jesus was the lamb offered as a blood sacrifice for the world to be blessed. Jesus bore all manners of evil so we can receive all the goodness of God. In exchange for punishment, we receive forgiveness for our sins. All sickness and disease are vanished by the healing power of God by faith. We received God's righteousness, counsel, and justices for the rejection, guilt, and shame that come against us. In exchange for poverty and lack, we receive wealth and prosperity. We receive truth instead of lies and condemnation. Jesus took on every curse, which is modern-day dysfunction and chaos, so we can be blessed and have every area of our life in order. Jesus died so we can live. He was buried, and when He rose on the third day, broke every natural law, sin, and bondage so we can know freedom. When we lay down our sins, we are laying down the bondage that keeps us bitter, resentful, hateful, and rebellious. Your acceptance of the atonement of the blood of Christ has set you free.

Isaiah 53:3-4

He was despised and rejected by mankind, a man of suffering, and familiar with pain. Like one from whom people hide their faces he was despised, and we held him in low esteem. Surely he took up our pain and bore our suffering, yet we considered him punished by God, stricken by him, and afflicted.

God says you will know them by their fruit (Matthew 7:20). The fruit of the Spirit of God are love, joy, peace, patience, goodness, kindness, self-control, faithfulness, and gentleness. What are you producing? Anything else outside of God, not a person, a thing, or the latest trend will give you the blessings and promises that are for you eternally. God's blessings and promises do not end, and His promises are true and perfect. God wants you to bear his character, image, and likeness. You are a representative of Christ Jesus (2 Corinthians 5:20). Change is hard. For some, it is an immediate transformation and for others, like me, it was gradual. The first step is knowing and being aware of our own transgression, not justifying our bad behaviors or blaming others for triggering our behavior. Remember we had a choice; we chose division and rebellion. We admit that our sin has affected our lives and those around us. We ask the Father to forgive us. Then we repent by changing our mind and direction to not be involved in those thoughts or behaviors that have caused devastation and division. What a blessing it is that the one and only true God helps us out of our own ignorance, guilt, and sin. God saves us from our misery to get us to a place of gladness and gratitude for all that He has done.

Father, I thank You for showing me what needs to change in my life. Your ways are good, and I seek what is right in Your eyes. I place ____ (whatever is toxic in your life) in my hands and give it to You. Holy Spirit penetrate my heart, break this bondage of ____ (name of the sin), and guide my steps to be a reflection of You. Show me Your way, truth and life. In Jesus's mighty name, Amen.

CHAPTER 3
WORSHIP

Psalm 100 (AMP)

Shout joyfully to the Lord, all the earth.

Serve the Lord with gladness and delight.
Come before His presence with joyful singing.

Know and fully recognize with gratitude that the Lord Himself is God;
It is He who has made us, not we ourselves [and we are His].
We are His people and the sheep of His pasture.

Enter His gates with a song of thanksgiving
And His courts with praise.
Be thankful to Him, bless and praise His name.

For the Lord is good;
His mercy and lovingkindness are everlasting,
His faithfulness [endures] to all generations.

What is worship? Worship is visible in your actions of attributing reverent honor, adoration, and homage to God, Jesus, and the Holy Spirit (the three persons of the Trinity). Most important to know is that worship is a lifestyle. Worship takes all of who you are, in everything that you believe that focuses our reverence to exalt God in spirit and in truth either individually or corporately within a church. Worship comes in different layers that become the makeup that makes a person's character or the essence of the church that is aligned with the character, image, and likeness of who God is.

Most people associate worship with music, singing and dancing to God, or meditation surrounded by candles or statues. Truth is God created you to be a worshiper unto Him, not objects or people, but Him who created you and the world. Worship comes in a few different ways but leads to the same divine significance. One act of worship is humbling yourself. Worship is founded in surrendering to Him by renewing your mind and changing your heart posture to position God as your source. Worship also comes in the form of service submitting to the obedience of God's commands and dedicating your life to a Kingdom purpose. In order for worship to even be of the greatest form, two things have to happen first. Thanksgiving, worship, and praise all three go hand-in-hand. You cannot have one without the other.

Worth - Ship; what is God's worth to you? Worship is to express adoration and honor to God regarded to the highest standard as Holy. Holy in Hebrew is *qodesh* means sacred, separate, and set apart. In the New Testament "holy" is the word *hagios*, which has the same meaning but also worthy of veneration; great respect, and reverence. When it comes to worship, it is what you pay sacred honor to. In the original Hebrew biblical text, the word for worship is *shachah*, which means to "be prostrate or bow down with your face to the ground." In the Greek text, worship is *proskyneō*, "kneeling or prostration to do homage (to one) or make obeisance (respect) shown to a superior rank." Worship is putting someone or something higher than you. But why?

The matter of motive to worship, praise and thanksgiving are very important. God wants and commands that we put Him as number one, putting God first in every area of our life, to have a Kingdom dominance over your life to produce and generate multiplication of blessings now and generationally. God is an eternal God. Your blessing rewards of putting God first will affect an overflow of blessings to your bloodline for generations but also your surroundings and when you leave this earth there are rewards in heaven. Look into your heart and ask what you "bow down" to. What is first in your life? God first, then everything will fall into place. *(Example: God first, then family/home, job/finance, other things/friendships)*. When you praise people or things higher than God, Jesus, and the Holy Spirit, it is a "false god," an idol that does not produce blessings, promises eternally, divine order, or alignment. A false god can be family, money, relationships, addictions, obsession, even ambitions, etc., anything that is first in your life before God causes a breach in the hedge of protection.

Matthew 6:33 NIV

"But seek first his kingdom and his righteousness,
and all these things will be given to you as well."

Music, singing, and dancing are forms of praise. In Hebrew, the words for praise are *halal* and *yadah,* which means to boast, confess, act foolish (celebration), glorify, and give thanks. It's where we get "Hallelujah" or "Praise the Lord." Giving the highest esteem or edifying is to praise.

When King David wrote Psalm 19, he looked at the creation, and although it says no words, just in who they are in the day-to-day, the earth and the clouds in the sky praise and worship God because God is the Creator of all things. Let everything that has breath praise the Lord (Psalm 150:6). That is a command. Our praise should be the highest praise to God that never fades. Our praise should be praise that magnifies His greatness that is continual. Praise is the gateway or key that opens the door to manifest God's presence (Psalm 22:3). God inhabits our praise, meaning He shows up. God does not show up in complaining; God shows up in our praising. We praise Him because we know that He is all things and will bless us *according to His will.* Praise declared with our mouth prepares the way for the supernatural intervention of who God is and what He has done on our behalf. We lift Him high with praise. Worship is our actions that is evidence that we believe that God is all things to us by faith as our top priority.

We cannot access God without the principle of applying thanksgiving to God. It is by God's grace (favor) we are thankful and show gratitude. His grace and mercy are new every morning. It's a key that unlocks the supernatural power of God. We are thankful we are activating our faith in Him. Our heart posture in the will of God is to always be thankful. The moment a person is out of the will of God is the moment they are not giving thanks to God because they have not acknowledged the fact that God's hand is in everything. God created everything including the mind of the individual who invented things (Colossians 1:16). God owns everything (Deuteronomy 10:14), so everything you have is because God gave it to you (1 Timothy 6:17).

By thanksgiving, we acknowledge God's goodness. By praise, we acknowledge God's greatness. By worship, we acknowledge God's holiness. The first four instructions in the Ten Commandments state God are number one: honor His name, worship God only, and keep the Sabbath day sacred as a time of meditation and reflection on what God has done in our lives, for the world, and what is to come. The Word says that we are to worship God in Spirit and in Truth but also to give thanks and praise while we are entering into His presence. How we worship in spirit, truth, and entering into the presence of God is our heart posture. The second is the declarations of our words. Last, our actions will reflect what the Word of God says. We cannot worship something we do not know. To know God is to read the everlasting Word of God. There is an infinite revelation of who God is; we have to seek Him, and He will show us through the Bible.

The best time to give thanks, praise, and worship is when we don't want to praise at all. When everything is going wrong. When we are under extreme pressure, especially unbearable sorrow. God says to cast our cares on Him because God cares for us (1 Peter 5:6-7). Be thankful; praise God for what he has done and is going to do. Let worship change our hearts in the roughest times, magnifying that God is greater than any situation. Complaining exposes Satan's attack on us; the more we talk about the situation, the more bitter, angry, and resentful we become. However, when we are speaking words of thankfulness, praise, and worship instead of the circumstance, we are inviting God into our current condition. This invitation is the key to God's victory and changes every situation for our good. This shows that we are trusting God to fight our battles. These types of thankfulness, praise, and worship are costly sacrifices because it takes everything in us to express thanks, praise, and worship in the worst of times. We are building the altar in our hearts that makes room for God to step into every area that needs healing or restoration. The bigger the trial, the bigger the blessing even if the blessing is divine correction (Hebrews 4:6-7). Let the storm come and praise Him for the victory! That is a spiritual weapon we use to silence and defeat the enemy; we know and believe God wins every time even if the enemy happens to be our fleshly nature. We speak the Word of God, which is truth. We are thankful that we have authority over any environment, and we are not defeated (2 Corinthians 4:8). If we see defeat that is a lie of the enemy. Wait in faith, do not react in fear, and watch God move. Praise God because we know and believe by faith that every promise is true. We will see the victory and restoration of every broken place in our life (Isaiah 45:2). We worship God because of His protection, deliverance, provision, healing, restoring, creative, and loving-kindness that He is (1 Samuel 12:22).

Proverbs 18:21 (NIV)

The tongue has the power of life and death,
and those who love it will eat its fruit.

Be careful what you say, because what you speak is what will happen. If you speak (complaint) disease, gossip, corruption, manipulation, hatred, poverty, bitterness, even fear - those are words of death. That is what you are calling to happen. Those who love to hear these words of death will associate you with those words you speak. You are either innocent or guilty by your words (Matthew 12:37). What comes out of your mouth is what is in your heart (Matthew 15:18). What you speak shall come to pass (Isaiah 55:11). It is a sin to speak against yourself and of other people. What are you calling your hardship moments? Failure or lessons? These negative words are not how God created us to be. God created mankind to be worshipers unto Him. He gave us words to speak to create by our words just like God did when He created the world (Genesis 2:19-20). When God said, "Let there be light," light came into being by His word. God kept creating by His words for six days creating the world and all that is within it by His words (Genesis 1). God called us as worshipers to create and call things that are not yet in existence (Romans 4:17). That is why we speak life and edification, not words that crush a spirit (Proverbs 15:4, Proverbs 12:18). The words on our lips are connected to our heart and were created to praise out of love (Psalm 19:14).

What we say about ourselves or others, "I am broke" or "they are broke," we are speaking curses unto ourselves or others (James 3:10). Those words are proclaiming poverty into being. How we reverse the curses we speak is when we speak and believe that we are prosperous, healed, forgiven, unified, in perfect peace, made whole, and confident with straightening to hold our head high - that is what is going to happen. It is not about what we feel. It is what we believe. These are the promises of God that we are speaking. That every broken and crooked place is being put back together (Luke 3:5, Isaiah 40:4) We give thanks, praise and worship to God, even if we do not see it at this moment, by faith we believe that it is going to happen (Matthew 21:22). That is the will of God for our life to speak and create a life of multiplication. We have to ask ourselves what do we want to multiply? Whatever "that" is, we speak "that" into existence. God wants to bless us and bless us abundantly. Make sure your words and actions align with the Word, character, and image of God. Thank God for all the changes in your life that are good, call the changes that were hard "great lessons." Praise God for what He has done, is doing, and going to do. Worship God because God alone, through the Holy Spirit that is within us, can change our thoughts, hearts, and words to speak what will happen. Our faith creates life by our words and the belief in our hearts that it will come to pass through God is a part of worship.

Philippians 4:8 (NIV)

Finally, brothers and sisters, whatever is true, whatever is noble, whatever is right, whatever is pure, whatever is lovely, whatever is admirable—if anything is excellent or praiseworthy—think about such things.

The key to worship is putting God first in every area of our life. First things first, your time, talent, and treasure. These three T's are what make up your daily functions for the first fruit harvest. "First fruits" in Hebrew is *bikkurim*, in English, it is the first ripe fruit for the altar of God and literally means "promise to come." In the Old Testament when the Israelites came before the Lord, they came with an offering which was the *bikkurim*, waving it before the Lord. What you do with your first hours of the day, your first actions, thoughts, the first portions of your finances are what governs what happens to the rest. Matthew 6:33 is important to understand because it is the key to everything. Seek

FIRST the Kingdom of GOD - then - all these things (God deems best as your proper and primary portion) will be added to you. In order to receive, we have to first give. God gives us a blessing in time, talent, and treasure. We don't take it and run; we give God back a portion of honor. Our "first" is the foundational root we build upon. This is the part of worship that is the service of our time, talent, and treasure. It is how we are giving to God what is due Him. The more we give back to God, the more blessings He gives us in return. For where our treasure is, there our heart will be also (Matthew 6:21).

Romans 11:16 NKJV

"For if the first fruit is holy, the lump is also holy; and if the root is holy, so are the branches"

Time

Time with God is super important. 3 John 1:2 tells us that God wants us to prosper in all things, even as our soul prospers. We are developing ourselves by putting God first in our time. God is prospering us in all things, including our souls by His Word, by our praise, by our obedience to answer His call to build for the Kingdom of God, and lastly, by the time we set ourselves apart in prayer and meditation with God alone. Daniel in the book of Daniel in the Bible prayed three times a day. He woke up early in the morning and prayed, at noon he prayed, and in the evening he prayed. Moses met God on Mount Sinai. Enoch and Noah walked faithfully with God alone, they spent their time with God enough to call them faithful friends. Adam walked in the cool of the day with God in the garden of Eden alone. God wants to communicate with you when you set your time apart for Him. Not just for fellowship but to receive revelation for relationship and mysteries to be imparted to you by God himself.

Luke 9:58 (NIV)

Jesus replied, "Foxes have dens and birds have nests, but the Son of Man has no place to lay his head."

The first instruction was for mankind to have authority over the earth and multiply (Gen. 1:26-31). God would meet Adam and Eve in the garden as a regulatory custom to communicate face to face. They spent time with God and talked with God. What kind of time are you giving to God? When Jesus said He had no place to rest His head, He was saying He had no place to reproduce His innovative ideas, strategies, concepts to multiply His instructions for Kingdom business that is to come through you. God can't give you plans if He doesn't communicate with you, and you will not receive divine strategies if you do not know Him (John 15:15). These are hidden treasures of wisdom and knowledge that you only get when you spend time with God.

Psalm 32:8 (NIV)

I will instruct you and teach you in the way you should go; I will counsel you with my loving eye on you.

Are you going to God first when making decisions? It is extremely important that you do. God's plans for us are to prosper, teach, and guide us in the right direction, have victory, and for our protection. All of God's counsel has a purpose and a reward. Sometimes people get in a position where they say, "Maybe the outcome would have been different if I would have prayed." When you go to God, He will say "Yes, that will bring you favor… No, don't go there... Release certain people, I have someone better." Sometimes God's counsel is even down to what you wear or how you speak to someone. It is our job to obey God's instructions, not to do our own thing that will lead to disorder and devastation. For example: God tells or prompts you first thing in the morning. "Wear that yellow shirt," God may say. You don't want to wear that but God, by His Holy Spirit is prompting you to wear the yellow shirt. There is a person you need to talk to, and they will say "I like that yellow shirt," and that is the person who is the key that will get you to your next assignment.

How you enter is just as important as how you exit a divine assignment. Be careful how you exit. How you exit one situation will determine the next. That is how you get repeated cycles and then you question, "Why does this keep happening?" When you lean on your own actions and thinking, not with God's counsel, the way YOU handled the situation led to devastation because it was not God's way. That is why you have to pray and ask God for direction and wait on God for the answer. Do NOT take matters into your own hands. While you wait, praise Him. God enters into your praise. While you praise you get peace. God will always look at your heart. If anything causes division in any way, that is not from God. A situation might have been bad but do not curse it, speak blessings as you enter and speak blessings as you leave.

First thing in the morning just say, "*Good morning, Holy Spirit, I would like to partner with you today, lead me to a word in the Bible that will sustain me all day. Let me be a vessel for you. Show me how I can share Your Word with the revelation You give me of Your heart and mind with others, so they too will be blessed.*" The more you study and spend time with God, the more you will transform and see that the Lord is good. Your actions and your words will reflect the image of who He is through the transformation of the Holy Spirit. The first part of your day will dictate the rest. The time you spend with God is the blueprint to the foundation of your life.

Talent

Every person has a gift or talent. Once you discover that gift, you have to practice that gift over and over to perfect your expertise. God will require you to use that gift for service toward his purpose and call on your life. Your gift and talent produce service, your service produces credibility, which develops into influence, that changes the atmosphere, and becomes a seed, that produces fruit and dominion. God wants you to be fruitful and multiply. Worship without service is hypocrisy; worship and service go hand in hand. They never separate. In order to do that you have to serve. How do you serve? Use the talent that God gave you.

Exodus 31:3 (NIV)

I have filled him with the Spirit of God, with wisdom, with understanding, with knowledge and with all kinds of skills—

There is a difference between service and desire. For example, there is a piano on a stage, some might have the desire to play it but only a few are skilled to play a concerto on the piano. David was called a man after God's heart. He would sing, write songs, and blow kisses to God while he was alone in the field tending sheep. God called David out of the field to the palace to play his music for King Saul who was tormented by evil spirits. When David played, the evil spirits would flee. David's gift made room for him to go into high places.

While Solomon was building the Temple, God picked those with special skills to build and design the perfect temple with the finest equipment. You might not be talented instrumentally. Can you bake? Make cookies for your prayer group and watch God open a door to a cookie business. Are you good at creating graphic design art? Ask to serve in your church in their marketing area. The more you use your talents for God's glory, He will open doors for you to step in and multiply you.

Treasure

A man's treasure can be summed up in a ton of things, such as money, family, home. Hannah gave her firstborn son unto the

Lord (1 Samuel 1-2:21). Hannah prayed from the depths of her soul because she was not able to produce any children. God opened Hannah's womb and bore a son named Samuel. Samuel was Hannah's treasure that God provided for her. Once her son was weaned, she took her son to the priest Eli for him to raise Samuel in the house of the Lord, and then she praised God. God blessed her with three more children. God multiplied her blessing of children because of what she did with her first child. Throughout the Bible, people gave more unto the Lord their very best. This best was their offering to the Lord and God multiplied their best offerings.

Deuteronomy 16:17

Each of you must bring a gift in proportion to the way the LORD your God has blessed you.

Has God blessed you? You have a roof over your head. You have shoes on your feet. You have a job. I heard this saying by quite a few ministers, "When you are down to your last dollar, do not spend it, sow it." Plant your seed into God's good soil. Meaning if you trust God who supplies all of your needs, by faith we release, "sow" that dollar to God, and not things, so that God can multiply what we give God to supply our need. Give Him the best offering.

Mark 4:19

but the worries of this life, the deceitfulness of wealth and the desires for other things come in and choke the word, making it unfruitful.

Knowing who and what God is to you, how you apply worship inward will determine how serious your worship is to Him. You must understand the gratitude of God's blessings. Even in the small graces, He gives you, those are the heart placement of what treasures you give to God. What you give God is a representation of who God is to you. If you put God first in your finances, God will take those "first fruit" offerings and bless it.

Genesis 28:20-22 (AMP)

Then Jacob made a vow (promise), saying, "If God will be with me and will keep me on this journey that I take, and will give me food to eat and clothing to wear, and if [He grants that] I return to my father's house in safety, then the Lord will be my God. This stone which I have set up as a pillar (monument, memorial) will be God's house [a sacred place to me], and of everything that You give me I will give the tenth to You [as an offering to signify my gratitude and dependence on You]."

Jacob put God first. He recognized that God is His provider in everything. God wants your first part of the day. Do you wake up and go to sleep praying and thanking God? The last thing Jacob said was about his finances. He recognized that whatever God gives Jacob, Jacob will give back to God the required ten percent that is the tithe for multiplication. Some people worship themselves. They see themselves as higher than they think they should and that their blessings were their own doing. God blessed you so you can be a blessing, has apportioned to each a degree of faith [and a purpose-designed for service]. Tithing is a part of worship; worship is a part of service and it comes with an open heaven blessing, meaning overflow. Do you tithe your first 10% of your gross income whenever your paycheck or any kind of money comes in? Even the best of businesses follows this biblical principle of giving back 10+% of their revenue to charity because they get a return on their contribution. Tax consultants will tell you, anyone who follows the tithe principle has shown an average of 30-60% increase in their income (Matthew 13:8). God blesses this principle whether they are a Christian or not. God's promises are true and never fail. When people wonder why non-Christians get blessed monetarily, more than likely they are following God's promised principles of giving. They gave a blessing somewhere and they receive blessings. God's promises always come to pass no matter who you are.

Malachi 3:8-12 (NIV)

"Will a mere mortal rob God? Yet you rob me.
"But you ask, 'How are we robbing you?'

*"In tithes **AND** offerings. You are under a curse—your whole nation—because you are robbing me. (that when you do not give God the tithe AND offering)*

*Bring the **WHOLE tithe** into the storehouse (Church), that there may be food in my house. **Test me** in this," says the Lord Almighty, "and see if I will not **throw open the floodgates of heaven** and **pour out so much blessing that there will not be room enough to store it.** I will **prevent pests from devouring your crops**, and the **vines in your fields will not drop their fruit before it is ripe**," says the Lord Almighty. "Then all the nations **will call you blessed**, for yours will be a **delightful land**," says the Lord Almighty.*

Bring God your tithe, offering, and financial seeds planted into God's Word - your financial treasure planted into the soil of His church (not your bills or pleasures) - THE WHOLE TEN PERCENT **AND** OFFERING **AND** SOW. Tithe: 10% of your gross income into the storehouse (your church). If you can bless and honor God's house, God will bless and honor your house. Give God what belongs to God and you keep the rest. You received $10, God gets $1, and you keep $9. God will bless your whole income ($10). Offering: is any extra amount that you give beyond your tithe. Sow: "reap what you sow," this is the financial seed of trust unto God, this is our investment in God, in His Word, our purpose that He planned for us; separate from the tithe and offering. Three principles of financial giving; the only place in the Bible that God says to test Him on His Word is through the tithe.

If someone says they do not have an income to give in tithe and offerings, put them on the evangelist team. Because "The fruit of the righteous is a tree of life, and he who wins souls is wise" (Proverbs 11:30). If their heart is to honor God, they will honor what God loves. If they can be trustworthy in bringing souls into the Kingdom of God, then they will be trustworthy to steward abundant finances. They don't have a monetary seed to give, but they can sow seeds in the Kingdom of God with their service of time and talent until they start producing an income. When they do what God says, watch God turn their life around. God will give them a job that supplies ALL of their needs, their home will get in order, their family will start coming to Christ. God will do a complete makeover on them if their heart is set to honor God, God will honor them. To receive we need to give; we need to give our seed to release our harvest. These three financial gifts of worship, the very BEST gifts of worship, go to God. When we give to God, it helps us grow in spiritual maturity, obedience, and the disciplines we need for protection and provision. Seed secures our future, opening the door to prosperity, into multiplication, healing for our bodies, and rebuking the lies of the enemy of poverty. Our seed of worship to God is powerful. There is increase and favor for us when we obediently give in the tithe, offering, and sow. Your heart is where your money is. God said He will supply all of our needs until it overflows. Basically, you have to give stuff away to make room for more. God will protect you. What God supplies you with will last eternally as long as you stay faithful to God's order. We cannot worship what we don't know, so start to magnify His name: God, You are my Provider, God, You supply all of my needs. Your transition is in the praises of His name. God's blessing will be attractive to people. That means God is blessing you to be a blessing. That is a part of worship.

2 Corinthians 9:6-7 (NASB)

The point is this: whoever sows sparingly will also reap sparingly, and whoever sows bountifully will also reap bountifully. Each one must give as he has decided in his heart, not reluctantly or under compulsion, for God loves a cheerful giver.

God loves a cheerful giver. The devil hates those that give to the church because he does not want us to prosper. When God starts blessing people with nice things, there will always be someone who comes along to try to downgrade their upgrade. The devil does not want to see the children of God prosper. The devil will always try to raise their debt. When people inherit a lot of money or win the lottery, all of a sudden people come out of nowhere who say they owe them money or people come to beg for money. It is funny that most people when they get in a good place, a bill comes out of nowhere on some sort of tax you missed. God does not want you to owe anyone. Matthew 22:21 Jesus said, "Render to Caesar the things that are Caesar's; and to God the things that are God's." Pay your taxes, pay your bills on time so you do not have to pay the extra taxes on late fees. Sow "up" (beyond your limit) there will be a thoughtful amount attached to your purpose that God says give in a way that will stretch your faith and financial plan, but you will receive back the fruit of thirty and sixty and a hundredfold harvest from that seed planted in God's time (Matthew 13:8). Sow "down" by helping someone in need so God will cover you in your necessities. Sometimes giving feels like a sacrifice, but if you reap sparingly you will receive sparingly. But if you give generously, you will receive a generous blessing.

Sacrifice

The sacrifice of worship comes with an extreme leap of faith, usually overcoming some sort of fear, or tears deep from the heart and incredible praise of thanks. This comes with putting our flesh aside and saying yes to God when everyone would have said no. Sometimes people will think you're crazy for submitting to this form of worship where you do not care what people think around you. It is these sacrifices of worship when the opposition says, "you are doing too much." God might say, bless your enemy. It might take all of your heart. Your pride might break in a deep way to sow into their business, but God will test your stewardship, honor, and faith toward relationship, covenant, and unity. These sacrifices of worship come with a great reward.

Jesus went to the Garden of Gethsemane the night before His crucifixion and prayed to God in tears till bloody sweat was dripping down his forehead. His life was the sacrifice on the cross for the whole world (Luke 22:44). Mary Magdalene, the sister of Martha and Lazarus broke an extremely expensive bottle of perfume worth a year's wage on Jesus's feet, wiped it with her hair, and kept kissing his feet with tears of passionate thanks of worship (Luke 7:38, John 12:1-11). The disciples started to condemn her, and the Pharisees kept bringing up her past sins (Luke 7:38). Jesus told them to leave her alone, she was forgiven. They did not know what she went through for her praise to be so bold. You cannot understand her praise until you read the chapters before. Jesus delivered her from seven demons (Luke 8:2) and raised her brother Lazarus from the dead (John 11). Not only that she loved Jesus so much, but her worship was also so passionate it made people uncomfortable. King David's wife Micah despised his praise when He was dancing and shouting for victory almost naked in front of a crowd. She focused and condemned David's behavior of his nakedness instead of seeing his expression of praise to God. David justified his praise to God by saying, "I will become even more undignified than this" for God's honor, and Micah had no children from that day forth (2 Samuel 6:14-23). This is unashamed worship to God. The kind of worship that is between you and God. The kind of worship that takes everything you have in your heart to release to God alone. The kind of worship that others might criticize or condemn because they do not understand the story behind your worship of your boldness to act in faith. This type of worship challenges our fear and will launch us into the next dimension. Start to transition, start to praise God, and magnify His name. This worship is your weapon against spiritual warfare. I have heard many people sow everything they had in their bank account because God asked them to do it, the sow was returned to them 100-fold. Some people have sown in tears. Some sown in shouts of praise. This is the very best worship when the worship takes us on another level of trust in God and rebuking the fear that paralyzes praise.

Father, help me to understand worship with a heart of gratitude and a heart hungry to praise you. I am submitting all of who I am to you for kingdom worship: my time, my talent, and my treasures so that it pleases you and the blessings multiply to be a blessing to others. I ask in Jesus's name, Amen.

CHAPTER 4
WHO IS GOD?

Isaiah 43:11-12 (NIV)

I, even I, am the Lord, and apart from me there is no savior. I have revealed and saved and proclaimed— I, and not some foreign god among you. You are my witnesses," declares the Lord, "that I am God."

I remember talking to this lady when I was learning who God is. She became Yoda from Star Wars, all of a sudden and said to me, "I am because God is." I looked at her like she was crazy. I replied, "What in the world are you talking about? What does that even mean?" Of course, she had the best intentions to impart some deep spiritual knowledge of God. That did not help me. If anything, it confused me even more. Who is God?

Trinity

The Trinity is God, Son (Jesus), and Holy Spirit, all three are conjoined together that makeup one eternal God in three persons. How are they three persons? God is the head of the Trinity. God the Father sent His, Son, Jesus, to fulfill the promise of eternal life by shedding his blood on the cross to close the gap of separation from sin that started in the Garden of Eden. After Jesus died and rose from the dead, He was alive, ministering to people for 40 days preparing them for the work of the Kingdom of God. When Jesus ascended into Heaven to be seated at the right hand of the Father, He sent the Holy Spirit to live inside of us so we can have a relationship with God as He did with Adam in the Garden of Eden from the beginning of earth's creation. Before, God would only speak to a priest who was purified and cleansed of sin by offering animals as a sacrifice of sin offerings to God. So, then a priest would go behind the veil in the Temple to communicate with God about the people and the nation. God sat on the Ark of the Covenant called the Holy of Holies (the most holy place). The priest would intercede for the people. The priest had bells on the bottom of his garment; anyone who was not authorized by God who stepped behind the veil would die because nothing unclean can step into God's presence. When Jesus died, He became the lamb-sin-sacrifice offering for the whole world. When Jesus died, the veil to the Holy of Holies was torn, so we can enter into God's presence through thanksgiving, praise, and worship. When Jesus rose from the dead, He ministered among the people for 40 days telling them they are now priests of the Kingdom of God and prepared them to do more works and share the Gospel with the whole world. Jesus sent a Helper to fulfill this task. Jesus sends the Holy Spirit to take dominion within us to do Kingdom work. Now our body is the temple that houses the Spirit of God. Since we house the Spirit of God, we have to keep ourselves pure and holy (set apart) for Kingdom work. So, we have to get rid of toxic things in our life to be disciplined with core values that are not double-minded. Now we must daily die to our sin by repentance, so the Holy Spirit to take dominion to transform us into the image, integrity, and purpose of God created for us in this time.

The Great I AM.

God alone is all things good, lovely, perfect, and just. God's existence is just that, I AM. I AM holds the key to dominion and victory. I AM is the authority in life itself. God is the great I AM. The Holy Spirit that lives inside of you gives you access to say I AM *whole,* I AM *provided for,* I AM *victorious,* I AM *rich,* I AM *content,* I AM *blessed,* I AM *healed,* and all the other things of who God is to you. Who is God to you? Once we ask in prayer to know the nature, character, and image of God for ourselves in a personal way, we will see that we can become the "I am" of God. What you think and declare to yourself you have to also believe it in your heart as well, otherwise your mind and heart will be in conflict. For example, if someone who operates in anger starts to say, "I will be kind" then makes the decisional actions to walk in kindness. They will eventually be able to say, "I am kind." Start speaking to yourself words of change. I am sober. I am financially free. I am smart. I am happy. I am business-minded... Make those "I will /can" choices to get to that place of "I am" in God. Never forget that God IS who you say you are. If you identify with 'poverty', poverty is not of God. Your identity is of Christ. When you are speaking an "I am" phrase. It is not about you. The I Am is the evidence of the transformation in your life that GOD has done. Do not stand on the fine line of being tempted to worshiping yourself. When you stop relying on God and start relying on yourself you are submitting to disobedience and rebellion. The "I Am" is because God allowed it your life so you can declare what God has done to bless you.

Kingdom of God

In the Old Testament, the Kingdom in its original Aramaic term is *malkut* and in the New Testament, the Kingdom is *basileia* in the Greek. It would be translated as OT: "Tree of Life" and the NT: "Rule of God." God has dominion on earth as it is in heaven in all creation. The way the Kingdom is mentioned in the Bible is to have primary rule and reign of a king for a kingdom. When Jesus came and he talked about the "Kingdom of God." Most people thought He was referring to taking dominion over the Roman Empire, but that was not so. He was talking about a Holy Nation with spiritual authority and ruler headship over evil rulers and principalities and spirits of darkness. God wanted people to understand and bring their concepts to a childlike sense because their concepts were brought up to a political sense. This was not a political campaign. It was very supernatural. He used parables and other methods to help the disciples and others understand what the Kingdom of God (Rule of God) is like. The Kingdom of God is the supernatural dominion of souls. God governs all things, it is

God's sovereign governance over you, me, and all creation (**Yahweh/YHWH**). David's Psalm gives a brief description of the Kingdom.

Psalm 103:19-22 (NIV)

The Lord has established his throne in heaven,
and his kingdom rules over all.

Praise the Lord, you his angels,
you mighty ones who do his bidding,
who obey his word.
Praise the Lord, all his heavenly hosts,
you his servants who do his will.
Praise the Lord, all his works
everywhere in his dominion.
Praise the Lord, my soul.

Abba=Father

Almost every Christian denomination can recite the "Lord's Prayer" It begins with saying "Our Father." *Abba* is the Aramaic equivalent for "father." Romans 8:15 expresses that you are a son of God. God has adopted you. When you are a child, you hold the genetic characteristics of your parents. God is saying you are my children, you hold the DNA characteristics of Him. He gives as a Father gives graciously to His children. He loves as a Father loves, He disciplines as a Father disciplines. He teaches as a Father trains a child. He is a compassionate Father: there is compassion covering over you and your household. God is the Head (dominion, rule, reign) of your household; God comes first in your home. The atmosphere of your home is a Kingdom atmosphere. As for me and my house, we serve the Lord (Joshua 24:15). It can be hard to grasp God the Father if you do not know what a good father or mother is supposed to be.

David in the Old Testament had the same problem. He was rejected by his father and brothers, an outcast to work as a shepherd in the fields. People questioned David's mother saying he was an illegitimate child, that he didn't matter. They cast David out as a good-for-nothing. David felt he only had God in this world, no friend, no family in a time of great need. Even when David became king, his children tried to take him down. Still, in David's abandonment, he wrote Psalm 27:10 saying - *Although my father and my mother have abandoned me, Yet the Lord will take me up [adopt me as His child].*

God is to you a Father, Mother, Friend (James 2:23), Husband (Isaiah 54:5), Shepherd (Psalm 23:1). God is your covering. Relationally where you were neglected, God supplies the need. God is like the song says, "Way Maker, Miracle Worker, Promise Keeper." God fills in the gap where you are empty and makes you whole. God loves you. You are the apple of God's eye (Psalm 17:8). Picture in your mind the most loving, caring, supportive parent or spouse; God is that to you AND MORE!! He will prove it. He is your Father, Friend, Covering, Husband. Those empty places of relationships, God is there to make you whole.

Jehovah Jireh = The Lord will Provide

Remember in the last chapter I mentioned giving your last dollar to the Lord and He will multiply it? That is basically it. God supplies your needs at just the right time because you trusted in the fact that God would provide or supply your needs.

Abraham had a son at an extremely old age named Isaac. God tested Abraham slightly differently from Hannah. Hannah willingly gave her son as an offering to the Lord and Samuel became one of the first and greatest prophets. Well, Abraham was instructed to give his son to God by a way of a sacrificial offering (he was going to kill him). Sounds crazy, I know.

Abraham obeyed, laid his son on the altar and as soon as Abraham was ready to sacrifice his son, God said STOP and pointed Abraham to an animal caught in the thickets, that is to be the sacrificial offering. So, Abraham named God Jehovah Jireh, The Lord Will Provide (Genesis 22:1-2; 9-10).

Have faith to give your treasure and believe that God will provide. Sometimes God will test you to see if you would 1) obey instructions and 2) trust Him. If you are poor and down to your last dollar, give God your dollar, He will supply a ride, food, clothing, rent. Give God all that you have, your tithe, your offering, the treasures in your heart for God to bless it because He is your Provider.

Jehovah- Shamah = Lord is there

In Ezekiel 48, during a time when God's people were in idolatry, God had withdrawn His presence, then Ezekiel has a vision of the Temple in Jerusalem in a glorious state. He sees God's presence returning to Jerusalem, the Temple restored not leaving it in ruins and comforted that God had not abandoned the Israelites who were His chosen people. God was there to rebuild the city and nation. The Israelites were not alone; His presence was there.

Jehovah-Rapha = God who heals

In the book of Exodus, the Israelites were wandering around the desert after they had left Egypt. They had all witnessed the ten plagues God put on Egypt. The Israelites were delivered from slavery, now in a barren land. They got to a river that was bitter. God had Moses throw a tree branch in the river to make it clean. Then God tells the Israelites: "*If you will diligently listen to the voice of the LORD your God, and will do that which is right in his sight, and will give ear to his commandments, and keep all his statutes, I will put none of these diseases on you, which I have brought on the Egyptians: for I am the LORD that heals you.*"

What does God heal you from? There are multiple verses in the Bible of God being a Great Physician. Jesus healed people from physically healing of blinded eye, deaf, and mute conditions (Mark 7:37, Matthew 9:27–31, Mark 8:22–26, John 9:1–41), or any ailments (Matthew 9:2–8; Luke 17:11–19). He heals the brokenhearted. God heals you from anxiety, God heals you from demonic spirits or spiritual fatigue. God can heal you from emotional suffering. God can heal you from your diseases, cancer, schizophrenia, and the demonic roots behind it. God heals you from whatever you need healing from. You say I AM healed. My vision is restored, my mouth can speak praises again, I can hear clearly, I can think clearly, I can breathe again. I AM WHOLE. Praise God, because He is your Healer!

Jehovah-Shalom= the Lord send "peace"

In the book of Judges 6:24, God finds Gideon hiding in fear and worry in a wine press and God calls Gideon a mighty warrior. God made Gideon a military leader, judge, and prophet that led the Israelites to victory. In the time of war, Gideon didn't ask for victory. He didn't ask for success or to make his name great after the win. Gideon asked God for peace. In the middle of this battle, he builds an altar and asks God for peace. The humility that Gideon showed exposed how great a leader God created Gideon to be. Gideon asks is for a nation to be absent from strife.

When you call on God, you are calling on Him to make you absent from strife. God steps in with his presence and brings a peaceful calmness in your heart to be at peace.

Jehovah-Nissi = The Lord is my banner

A banner is a sign of victory. This is what Moses was saying. My victory is in God. The Israelites fought a great battle against Amalek. As long as Moses kept the rod raised high (the same rod that parted the Red Sea) the Amalekites would flee. Moses after this great battle had built an altar to the Lord and dedicated the altar to the victorious God for Israel's triumph (Exodus 17:15). An altar implies a sacrifice, in this case, it was a sacrifice of praise that the battle was won under God's leadership (his banner of victory). Rise your banner of victory to God who fights your battles for you to live victoriously (Exodus 14:14, Deuteronomy 1:30).

Psalm 46:1

God is our ***refuge*** *and* ***strength,*** *an ever-present* ***help*** *in trouble.*

God is there. He reminds you that He will never leave you or forsake you. He is your help; He will guide you. God was there before time began and He is here right now. He will still be with your children and their generations until the end of time. David said God is my **refuge**, God is my **strength**, and God is my **help**. Three very important things. Refuge meaning my shelter of safety. God is a protector. He will shield you. Of course, you might see things going on around you, but nothing can harm you. God gives you strength. David went through a lot of heart-wrenching things. He turned to God for strength. The Bible says the joy of the Lord is my strength (Nehemiah 8:10). Joy doesn't mean happiness. Happiness is a feeling; joy is a spirit. You can still have joy even though you are not happy. There are times when the weight is so heavy that you need strength to get out of bed and start a new day. God is your refuge, God is your strength, and God is your help. God sees and knows everything. What caught you by surprise did not catch God by surprise. God is saying to you "I got this," God is your helper when you call on His name.

El Emunah = The Faithful God

God keeps his promises. He is faithful (Deuteronomy 7:9), unlike people who say one thing and do another. God is not like that. God says let there be light and there was light. God says you are prosperous, believe Him. God says you are strong and courageous, believe Him. God is faithful to turn your situations around. God is faithful to bless, and God is faithful to give you purpose. God is faithful to be fruitful and multiply. God is faithful to answer your prayers. Start expecting God to answer your prayers, and do not be shocked when God supplies your need better than you asked because God is faithful to answer and provide. Be expecting that God is faithful.

Isaiah 9:6

For to us a child is born, to us a son is given, and the government will be on his shoulders. And he will be called ***Wonderful Counselor, Mighty God, Everlasting Father, Prince of Peace.***

I love this verse because it does not just name the names of Jesus, but it shows who He is. Wonderful is *pele,* which means miracle. Counselor is *yaats*, which means resolve. God will miraculously resolve your situation. He settles your dispute. Then not only that He is a mighty God. Mighty is the word *gibbor*, which means warrior. God is fighting your battles. It gets better… Everlasting Father, *ad* means perpetuity, there is no end, always, forever your Father in heaven. Prince of Peace... Peace here is *shalom*, it says safe, well, happy, friendly, welfare, health, prosperity, peace. All of this greatness is who God is and who He is to you. God is your source. He supplies all of your needs.

John 4:24

God is spirit*, and his worshipers must worship in the Spirit and in truth."*

1 John 1:5

God is light; *in him there is no darkness at all.*

1 John 4:8

Whoever does not love does not know God, because ***God is love****.*

John 1:1

In the beginning was the Word, and the Word was with God, and the ***Word was God.***

John talks about the nature of God. God is "full of grace and truth." John talks about God differently from all the other Gospel writers. People say they talk to God. They opened up their Bible and read the Word of God. The Bible is God's words *(dabar)* that speak to and through you. His word (*logos*) is either informing you or His word (*rehma*) is transforming you. In His word there is tangibility. God is love. His word activates the Holy Spirit inside you to transform because God is *Spirit* by using you as His vessel to speak forth His words to release an activation of a tangible reality. God came as flesh, sending His son Jesus, and Jesus ascended into heaven and sending the Holy Spirit of God to live in you. No longer in a temple but in your body, which is now the temple of God. That is why God wants you to keep yourself holy and pure. You wouldn't want the Queen of England or the President of the United States with all their reporters entering into your home that is dirty and messy for the world to see? The world sees what is inside of you. They see your heart, if your heart is not pure; how can God dwell and move if you keep blocking God access, with all your junk and rebellion? If you don't clean your heart, the Holy Spirit will prune and cut what doesn't belong and it will hurt, it might seem messy for a moment. Let go and let God do his good work in you.

Exodus 34:6-7

And he passed in front of Moses, proclaiming, "The Lord, the Lord, the ***compassionate and gracious God, slow to anger, abounding in love and faithfulness, maintaining love to thousands, and forgiving wickedness, rebellion, and sin.***

Yet he does not leave the guilty unpunished; he punishes the children and their children for the sin of the parents to the third and fourth generation."

Exodus 34:14

Do not worship any other god, for the ***Lord, whose name is Jealous****, is a* ***jealous God****.*

Moses was on Mount Sinai ready to write the Ten Commandments. God appeared to Moses revealing to Moses who He is, and that God wanted to make a covenant with Moses and the Israelites. He said this is all of my traits, oh and by the way, I'm jealous so do not put anything before me, put God first. You're mine and I'm yours and that is the covenant. This marriage is a sealed deal with no divorce. A covenant is exactly that, an agreement or a bound contract based on a relationship. God is saying I'll do this and be this for you if you do that which God commands. What God commands is always for your good and a purpose. Everything else outside of God's plan will be destroyed, in other words, it will not work. It is not just you; it is you and your children and their children, it is generational.

Revelation 1:8

"I am the ***Alpha and the Omega,"*** *says the Lord God, "who is, and who was, and who is to come, the* ***Almighty."***

Isaiah 44:6

Thus says the LORD, the ***King and Redeemer*** *of Israel, the* ***LORD of Hosts*** *(army angles): "I am the* ***first and I am the last,*** *and there is no God but Me.*

Alpha is the first letter of the Greek alphabet and *omega* is the last letter. These verses are explaining God's authority and his eternal divinity having all knowledge of time, history, and future from beginning to end. God is first from the beginning of time and the end of time that God brings everything to a complete and glorious conclusion. God works everything out for the good of those who love him (Romans 8:28). He saw your whole life. He knew how everything happened and also orchestrated every situation to work out for your good. God assigns angels to protect you and help in fighting your battles. He knows the paths you should take. No one comes to the Father except through Jesus. He steps in and says look, I covered this person with my blood, I see my son Jesus, your intercessor. God has the authority and dominion; what He starts He finishes. God is saying I got you and I got this, I know how it is going to end.

The angels around the throne sing praises to God day and night saying, "**Holy Holy Holy, You are Lord God Almighty**" (Revelation 4:6, 7:11, Isaiah 6:3). The angels around the throne of God spend eternity praising, worshiping, and magnifying His majesty stating that God is not only separate and completely different from everyone and anything else but that He is awesome. The magnificence of God, the *Shekinah* Glory is an overwhelming supernatural atmosphere of His splendor, brilliance, and adoration of God that subjects everything into order for the purpose of worship and awe. Dr. Danny DiAngelo always taught that "God is the only one worthy of reverence or ultra-high respect and admiration to be called awesome." Awesome means to be in awe, reverence, admiration. God's creation has in every age proclaimed the Trinity of God's eternal holiness. When you get to heaven, you too will be joining in on this choir of praise.

A list of names and verses of the second person of the Trinity: **Jesus = Son of God**.

Bread of Life *(Source of spiritual nourishment through the word and mouth of God)* John 6:35 (NIV)

Then Jesus declared, "I am the bread of life. Whoever comes to me will never go hungry, and whoever believes in me will never be thirsty."

Light of the World *(authority to make manifest, evident, exposed or clear, illuminate)* John 8:12 (NIV)

When Jesus spoke again to the people, he said, "I am the light of the world. Whoever follows me will never walk in darkness *(moral evil) but* will have the light of life."

The Door *(opportunity for salvation, growth, increase / deliverance into security)* John 10:9 (NIV)

I am the gate; whoever enters through me will be saved. They will come in and go out and find pasture.

Good Shepherd *(individual watchfulness, feeder, protector, and ruler of a flock of men who is fair, noble, morally excellent with tender care in his self-sacrificing love)* John 10:11, 14-18 (NIV)

I am the good shepherd. The good shepherd lays down his life for the sheep. I am the good shepherd; I know my sheep and my sheep know me—just as the Father knows me and I know the Father—and I lay down my life for the sheep. I have other sheep that are not of this sheep pen. I must bring them also. They too will listen to my voice, and there shall be one flock and one shepherd. The reason my Father loves me is that I lay down my life—only to take it up again. No one takes it from me, but I lay it down of my own accord. I have authority to lay it down and authority to take it up again. This command I received from my Father.

Resurrection and Life *(Revelation of divine authority over life and death / union to have: authority of perfect victory over corruption & eternal life)* John 11:25-26 (NIV)

Jesus said to her, "I am the resurrection and the life. The one who believes in me will live, even though they die; and whoever lives by believing in me will never die. Do you believe this?"

The Way, the Truth and the Life *(The only Mediator between God and man is Christ: way: passage of access | truth: cannot lie | life: being one with God eternal union and communication on earth as it is in Heaven)* John 14:6 (NIV)

Jesus answered, "I am the way and the truth and the life. No one comes to the Father except through me."

The Vine *(Union with Jesus; cultivate & increase discipleship, true followers, representatives of the Kingdom of God)* John 15:5 (NIV)

"I am the vine; you are the branches. If you remain in me and I in you, you will bear much fruit; apart from me you can do nothing" *(separation to all Christlike conduct =withering of manhood).*

Lastly, the third person of the Trinity: **Holy Spirit**

Ruach pronounced roo'-akh: wind or breath of God. The attributes of the Holy Spirit are the fruits of the spirit and the gifts of the spirit which we will talk about in the next chapter. *Ruach* of God is the divine energy of the gifts performed through you, the signs and wonders that you operate in by the Holy Spirit. For example: Genesis 1:2 (NIV) "Now the earth was formless and empty, darkness was over the surface of the deep, and the **Spirit of God was hovering (waiting to create at the sound of a command) over the waters.**" As soon as God spoke the command "Let there be light," the powerful energy force of the Holy Spirit for six days created the whole earth at the sound of God's command. At every "God said" the

Holy Spirit worked into reality, giving the command an eternal life to what God commanded.

Holy Spirit is a **helper** (John 14:26). The Holy Spirit comes in to convict our hearts for the purpose of repentance, also instilling in us divine works and mysteries for the edification of the Kingdom of God. The Holy Spirit gives us confirmation that we are a child of the living God. The Holy Spirit helps us to conform to the image of God, His character, and His likeness so that we can be his vessel and witness to the whole world. The Holy Spirit is the provision of our holiness and supplication on our behalf (Romans 8:26-27).

Ephesians 1:13-14 (NIV)

And you also were included in Christ when you heard the message of truth, the gospel of your salvation. When you believed, you were marked in him with a seal, the promised Holy Spirit, who is a deposit guaranteeing our inheritance until the redemption of those who are God's possession—to the praise of his glory.

The Old Testament is the works of God, and the Gospels are the works of Jesus. Acts and beyond are the works of the Holy Spirit. There are so many names of God, Jesus, and the Holy Spirit throughout all 66 books of the Bible for every need that you ask God to be for you. He will answer with His name, with His hand, with His works, and with His presence. Whatever name He is, He will always reveal His goodness toward you, His mercy toward you, and His covering over you.

"Know therefore that the Lord your God, He is God, the faithful God, who keeps covenant and mercy with them who love Him and keep His commandments to a thousand generations."

- Deuteronomy 7:9

CHAPTER 5
GIFTS FROM GOD

Matthew 7:16 (NIV)

By their fruit you will recognize them.

Fruit of the Spirit (Galatians 5:22-23) with the original Greek meaning:

- Love (*agapē*)
  - Ultimate love that is unconditional.
- Joy (*chara*)
  - Calm delight, cheerful contentment. Not happiness, happiness is a feeling that comes and goes. Joy is a holy exultation that arises from a sense of God's mercy.
- Peace (*eirēnē*)
  - Quiet justification in the soul, assurance of pardon, satisfaction to the mind, reconciliation with God
- Patience (*makrothymia*)
  - Withholding the assertion of our own rights, we are patient under long sufferings, perseverance and endurance
- Kindness (*chrēstotēs*)
  - A very rare grace of God. Implying sweetness of speech and manners
- Goodness (*agathōsynē*)
  - A benevolent and beneficent disposition, with all that is kind, soft, winning, and tender
- Faithfulness (*pistis*)

  - Fidelity - punctuality in performing promises, trustworthy of integrity

- Gentleness (*prautēs*)

  - Patient suffering of injuries without feeling a spirit of revenge, an even balance of all tempers and passions

- Self-control (*enkrateia*)

  - Sober 'self-mastery', abstinence of gratifications, a firm control over wicked passions attained to by moral discipline

These nine fruits of the Spirit are the character of the Holy Spirit imparted to believers in Christ as children of God inheriting evidence of graces in action within us. The Holy Spirit is a person, living inside of us dwelling and hovering over our hearts, just like in Genesis 1 waiting for the command of our words to be activated to create through prayer. These fruits grow within us by the operation of the Holy Spirit transforming our DNA to reflect the character of God. All of these nine fruits live in you. The Holy Spirit constantly works to rid our lives of the acts of sinful fleshly nature. You call on the Holy Spirit to help you walk in these fruits so that it starts to show in your character. We are to emulate the fruits of the Spirit daily, grow into their characteristics and transform daily into whom God wants us to become for His Kingdom glory.

1 Corinthians 14:26

"All of these must be done for the strengthening of the church"

There are many great teachings on the gifts of the Holy Spirit and how many gifts vary depending on teachings. "Now concerning spiritual gifts, brothers, I do not want you to be uninformed" (1 Corinthians 12:1). God wants you to know that He has gifts for you. Gifts are different from talents. Gifts and talents are different from the function of the five offices of the ministry. The office of the ministry is the foundation. You need all five offices for a great ministry to thrive. The gifts that God gives you are for the function of the church. Everyone is given different gifts. All of it together is for the strengthening of the church. All of it is for the Kingdom of God.

Your natural talent is something that you genetically inherited from your parents or were well trained in something with years and hours of work to perfect the talent. Some people sing, dance, paint, play sports, develop businesses, or do something that makes them unique. Some people discover their talents at a young age and some later on in life. However, when your natural talent is given and discovered, it is to be used to bless God. A spiritual gift is divinely given, imparted by the Holy Spirit for your work in the Kingdom of God. The gifts that are imparted to you by God are unique to your purpose for His glory. Nonetheless, gifts and talents produce service of worship and adoration to God.

Ephesians 4:11-12

So Christ himself gave the apostles, the prophets, the evangelists, the pastors and teachers, to equip his people for works of service, so that the body of Christ may be built up

This is called the offices of the "Five-Fold Ministry" chosen for a certain few and should be highly respected for the work in the Kingdom of God that they are held accountable. Their spiritual battles are different because of what they hold sacred. To build an effective ministry, you have to start with the five offices of ministry as a foundation. These are for those chosen into servant leadership based on their maturity and their level of authority. The lifestyle, public and private, of those who operate in the offices of ministry are extremely important. The leadership who holds the Five-Fold Ministry Offices are very careful not to indulge in the things of this world, so they might denounce others in moments of correction. Most live very disciplined or isolated lives. They do not accept or tolerate the wickedness of the world. A church that operates in all five is the most effective.

1. **Apostles:** This is the person in charge of the church. They usually govern and provide a spiritual covering over multiple churches in a region or nation. They are graced to build a church and have the authority to build and place people for the function of the church. They do not operate in favoritism but as serious master-builders of the foundation, order, theology, doctrine, and principles of the church structure and leadership. Once the foundation is made, they move on and build again. This is usually the one who suffers the most test and trials and spiritual warfare because of their responsibility.

2. **Prophets:** These are divine messengers. They see and speak the mind and heart of Christ. God gives them divine secrets and strategies of the Kingdom for the church, a community, and a nation. It will always align with scripture. They bring order and interact with angels. They have divine visions and dreams that are clear and precise for intercession with prayer and fasting. They suffer a long period of waiting to hear God until the appropriate time. When revelation comes, the messages hold a heavy weight. That is why not everyone is a prophet. Not everyone can handle the weight of the revelation message God gives them to deliver to a church, a community, or a nation. They must deliver and interpret the vision how God shows them.

3. **Evangelists:** These are soldiers on a mission to save and deliver people from hell and demonic oppression. They usually have a team ready to go into spiritual warfare. They have access to places that are usually overlooked, or nobody wants to enter. They bring the freedom of the Gospel. They train disciples to minister Christ's salvation. They seek and gather lost souls. They travel and search for revival, perform miracles, signs, and wonders in desolate places. They are often misunderstood and suffer persecution publicly because the strong discernment they carry brings conviction to hardened hearts, snatching people out of demonic bondage by exposing and uprooting sin.

4. **Pastors:** They are the shepherds of the flock to gather, protectors of souls, and guardians of the church body. They invest time with their congregation, usually a sphere of influence. They lead with unity and impart encouragement to the body of Christ. They counsel, equip, and lead individuals from brokenness to purpose. The burden they carry is for the hearts of each of their sheep equally and the church itself.

5. **Teachers:** They are called to break down the Bible either in a classroom, pulpit, in a written book, or by example. Their mission is to train people in biblical truth and make it understandable and applicable in their students' lives. They are constantly studying and dissecting scriptures. Their burden is finding people hungry enough to go into deep things of God.

1 Corinthians 12:28 New International Version (NIV)

And God has placed in the church first of all apostles, second prophets, third teachers, **then (after that)** *miracles, then gifts of healing, of helping, of guidance, and of different kinds of tongues.*

Now that the church is established, the Holy Spirit provides divine gifts for people to operate in and serve in the ministry. It is very important that you understand that your gifts and talents are not to be used for selfish gain. They are for the work of the Kingdom of God.

1 Corinthians 12:4-7

There are different kinds of gifts, but the same Spirit distributes them. There are different kinds of service, but the same Lord. There are different kinds of working, but in all of them and in everyone it is the same God at work. Now to each one the manifestation of the Spirit is given for the common good.

Gifts of the Spirit

1. **Support Gifts:**

    - Helps

        – 1 Corinthians 12:28 And God has appointed in the church first apostles, second prophets, third teachers, then miracles, then gifts of healing, helping, administrating, and various kinds of tongues.

    - Unity

        – Romans 1:12 That is, that I may be comforted together with you by the mutual faith both of you and me.

  - Romans 15:5 May the God who gives endurance and encouragement give you the same attitude of mind toward each other that Christ Jesus had,

- Mercy
  - Romans 12:8 if it is to show mercy, do it cheerfully.
- Encouragement
  - Romans 12:8 if it is to encourage, then give encouragement
- Giving
  - Romans 12:8 if it is giving, then give generously
- Hospitality
  - 1 Peter 4:9-10 Offer hospitality to one another without grumbling. Each of you should use whatever gift you have received to serve others, as faithful stewards of God's grace in its various forms.
  - Romans 12:13 Share with the Lord's people who are in need. Practice hospitality.
- Service
  - Romans 12:7 if it is serving, then serve
- Joy
  - 1 Thessalonians 1:6 You became imitators of us and of the Lord, for you welcomed the message in the midst of severe suffering with the joy given by the Holy Spirit.

- Intercession
  - 1 Timothy 2:1-2 I urge, then, first of all, that petitions, prayers, intercession and thanksgiving be made for all people for kings and all who are in high positions, that we may lead a peaceful and quiet life, godly and dignified in every way.

2. **<u>Teaching Gifts:</u>**

- Wisdom
  - Colossians 1:9 We continually ask God to fill you with the knowledge of his will through all the wisdom and understanding that the Spirit gives,
- Knowledge
  - 1 Corinthians 12:8 To one there is given through the Spirit a message of wisdom, to another a message of knowledge by means of the same Spirit,
- Understanding
  - Colossians 1:9 We continually ask God to fill you with the knowledge of his will through all the wisdom and understanding that the Spirit gives
- Teachings
  - Romans 12:7 if it is teaching, then teach
- Revelation
  - Ephesians 1:17 I keep asking that the God of our Lord Jesus Christ, the glorious Father, may give you the Spirit of wisdom and revelation, so that you may know him better.

3. **<u>Administrative Gifts:</u>**

    - Faith

        – 1 Corinthians 12:9 to another faith by the same Spirit, to another gifts of healing by that one Spirit,

    - Leadership

        – Romans 12:8 if it is to encourage, then give encouragement; if it is giving, then give generously; if it is to lead, do it diligently; if it is to show mercy, do it cheerfully.

    - Administration

        – 1 Corinthians 12:28 And God has appointed in the church first apostles, second prophets, third teachers, then miracles, then gifts of healing, helping, administrating, and various kinds of tongues.

4. **<u>Outreach / Missionary Gifts:</u>**

    - Witnessing Power

        – Acts 1:8 But you will receive power when the Holy Spirit comes on you; and you will be my witnesses in Jerusalem, and in all Judea and Samaria, and to the ends of the earth.

        – When it comes to having the "power to witness" is having the authority and help of the Holy Spirit to tell people about the resurrection, teachings, and works of Jesus according to scripture.

- Tongues
  - 1 Corinthians 12:10 to another miraculous powers, to another prophecy, to another distinguishing between spirits, to another speaking in different kinds of tongues, and to still another the interpretation of tongues.
- Interpretation
  - 1 Corinthians 12:10 to another miraculous powers, to another prophecy, to another distinguishing between spirits, to another speaking in different kinds of tongues, and to still another the interpretation of tongues.
- Discernment
  - 1 Corinthians 12:10 to another miraculous powers, to another prophecy, to another distinguishing between spirits, to another speaking in different kinds of tongues, and to still another the interpretation of tongues.
  - Discernment is NOT suspicion, never say "God said" unless you are 100% sure. Test what you are feeling, you have to wait for God. He will confirm either by the Word of God, visions, or by signs. It will oppose the flesh. It is the same with the gifts of prophecy. These two work hand in hand.

5. **Signs & Wonders Gifts:**

- Miracles
  - 1 Corinthians 12:10 to another miraculous powers, to another prophecy, to another distinguishing

between spirits, to another speaking in different kinds of tongues, and to still another the interpretation of tongues.

- 1 Corinthians 12:28 And God has appointed in the church first apostles, second prophets, third teachers, then miracles, then gifts of healing, helping, administrating, and various kinds of tongues.

- Healing
  - 1 Corinthians 12:28 And God has appointed in the church first apostles, second prophets, third teachers, then miracles, then gifts of healing, helping, administrating, and various kinds of tongues.

- Prophecy
  - Romans 12:6 We have different gifts, according to the grace given to each of us. If your gift is prophesying, then prophesy in accordance with your faith.
  - 1 Corinthians 12:10 to another miraculous powers, to another prophecy, to another distinguishing between spirits, to another speaking in different kinds of tongues, and to still another the interpretation of tongues.

- Deliverance
  - Acts 8:6-7 When the crowds heard Philip and saw the signs he performed, they all paid close attention to what he said. For with shrieks, impure spirits came out of many, and many who were paralyzed, or lame were healed.

"God's gifts and His calling are irrevocable" (Romans 11:29). No matter what you have done or what has been done to you, God will never revoke or take away His calling on your life or the gifts that He has given you to accomplish your calling. Anointed: you are called, chosen to the gift that will be used through you for God's purpose. God is a God of order. God blesses order and fruitfulness. When you try to use your gifts and call for the world or selfish gain. It will eventually backfire horrendously. You can be as gifted and talented as you want to be, but if the anointing is not there you are performing for yourself and not for the service of the Kingdom of God. Most of your gifts will activate (*anoint/flow*) only at the time it is needed. Some have to develop in gifts learning the right and wrong way to use them. If you have a great leader or mentor who recognizes your gift or call, they will help guide and teach you how to use your gift. If you are around people who recognize your gift and call and don't want you to develop or don't want you to freely operate in your gift and call or do not want to teach you, you are going to have a really hard time being suppressed. Your gift at the proper time is going to want to spring forth. In that case, pray and ask God to lead you to the right people, right leadership, right teachers to help you develop in the right way. That is why it is always good to surround yourself with the right people, get in the right church, under the right leadership. Get around people who are already doing and established in their gift and call that is similar to yours. See if they can take you under their wing. Find workshops and books on the subject and learn to develop yourself, too. What God gives you, invest in it.

CHAPTER 6
DREAMS VS SELFISH AMBITION

Habakkuk 2:2 (NIV)

Then the LORD replied: "Write down the revelation (vision) and make it plain on tablets so that a herald may run with it.

Dreams and ambitions are connected to your call through signs and symbols that are divinely given to you by God that lead you in the way of your purpose. There is a difference between God's desires and your desires. When God gives you a vision, it is for His purpose to take Kingdom dominion and authority for order and generational multiplication, a domino effect for the greater good. You should keep that vision in front of you at all times until it comes to pass. Desires that come from yourself are not from God; God cannot bless selfishness. A selfish dream will glamorize the lust of eye, flesh, and pride that will not multiply a blessing but a destructive and temporary success. God is a continual person. Once God starts something, it has no end.

God gave Joseph a dream. Joseph was the son of Jacob and one of twelve brothers. Joseph was Jacob's favorite son and was blessed with a coat of many colors that the other brothers hated. The first dream he said to his brothers, "Listen to this dream I had: We were binding sheaves of grain out in the field when suddenly my sheaf rose and stood upright, while your sheaves gathered around mine and bowed down to it" (Genesis 37:6-7). His brothers hated him even more. Then God gave Joseph another dream and he went and told his brothers again, "Listen," he said, "I had another dream, and this time the sun and moon and eleven stars were bowing down to me" (Genesis 37:9). Long story short, Joseph's brothers tried to kill him. They threw him in a pit and sold Joseph for twenty shekels of silver to the Ishmaelites, who took him to Egypt. Then Joseph was sold again to Potiphar, one of Pharaoh's officials in Egypt, and performed great service in his home. Potiphar's wife lies about Joseph saying he wanted to sleep with her. He ends up in jail. You see no matter where Joseph was, the Lord was with Joseph and gave him success in the works of his hands. The chief cupbearer and the baker of the king of Egypt ended up in jail with Joseph and needed a dream interpreted. The chief cupbearer and the baker were going back to the king and Joseph requested to mention him to Pharaoh and get him out of prison. Of course, they forgot about him. Two years passed, and Pharaoh had a dream, then chief cupbearer remembered Joseph. Joseph interpreted Pharaoh's dream, so Pharaoh put Joseph in charge of the whole land of Egypt. For seven years, Joseph stored an abundance of food before the famine came to pass. The famine was so severe that Joseph's brother traveled to Egypt to get food. So, when Joseph's brothers arrived, they bowed down to him with their faces to the ground not knowing the high official was their brother whom they sold for twenty shekels. When Joseph saw his brothers, he remembered his dream and wept. Joseph revealed himself to his brothers. The best thing about it was Joseph forgave his brothers and said it was God's plan (Genesis 50). God sent Joseph ahead of his family to preserve for them as a remnant on earth and to save their lives by a great deliverance from the famine. The dream that God gave Joseph came to pass.

Your ambition and drive should be that of the plan of the Kingdom of heaven. God is not going to tell you to join the circus, UNLESS, He plans for you to use that platform for His Kingdom glory. When God gives you a dream you better take it and run with it. You know it is God's plan because it will always bless you AND be a blessing for others. There is multiplication in the dream. Your ambition is to fulfill the call designed for you to accomplish. God gives you a vision, now you must put the vision into action. If you have to illegally take matters into your own hands, force things to go your way and manipulate people or a situation to get what you want, your heart is in the wrong place. Selfishness causes messy antics with discorded schemes to get ahead. God does not compete; you don't have to chase after it, manipulate, or push people out of the way to get God's blessings. You will eventually see the fruit of your obedience or selfishness. God weighs the heart and deals with you accordingly to your actions (Proverbs 24:12).

Romans 4:17

*As it is written: "I have made you a father of many nations." He is our father in the sight of God, in whom he believed--**the God who gives life to the dead and calls into being things that were not.***

Commitment

The greatest leaders apply this scripture to their lives and don't even know it. They call things that are not happening yet into existence. The law of attraction is biblical. The most successful people make a vision board. They keep the vision in front of them and make it happen. First, you need to know what God wants. Ask yourself does this align with God's Kingdom order? Write clear goals down. Cut out pictures of what you would like to happen in every area of your life. Make a plan from start to finish. Ask God, how do I get there? Let's make it happen! Use your faith and call those things that are not. Put your dream in order with an action plan. If you do not know how to put things in order, start with making your bed in the morning. Go through your clothes and organize them. Throw out what does not fit. Color coordinate things. Get your Tupperware in order in your kitchen. Put in order what you can see. These simple steps help your life get into order alignment so you can make room for what God has for you.

Luke 16:10-12

Whoever can be trusted with very little can also be trusted with much, and whoever is dishonest with very little will also be dishonest with much. So if you have not been trustworthy in handling worldly wealth, who will trust you with true riches? And if you have not been trustworthy with someone else's property, who will give you property of your own?

Back door access

I don't know nor will I pretend to know what it is like to have people hand me success or rub elbows to get in somewhere. I came in through the back door, watched and observed the operations, jumped in, and got my hands dirty. I didn't have a good education. I didn't know how to read or write or talk properly. I had to teach myself basic skills as a teenager. You knew where I came from the moment I opened my mouth. But I worked in visuals. I became a watcher of people, I learned, and then mimicked what I saw others do. Eventually, I ended up going back to school for formal education.

I loved PBS because they showed factories and operations. They showed you how a peanut gets crushed into a paste, put in a jar, labeled, packaged, shipped to a store then onto your kitchen for a topping on your breakfast toast. Operation, process, and order. When I had to learn how to fix my beat-up car on my own, I went to sleep learning how a car operates. I saw the connection between how the wheels turn when this part moves together with another. It was the same on a job. Process and order will always rise above disorder and that is how things operate smoothly. Pray for opportunities for God to show you order and blessings in your life (job, school, project, etc.).

A person once told me, "Fake it until you make it." I mimicked until I knew the rules, order, and process. All I knew was to say yes, then figure it out. Listen, watch, and learn from people how they got to the top. Study their day-to-day activities, gestures, and habits. Take pieces from people on the things they do that you noticed that make them a great leader and incorporate them into your daily life. For me, it was analyzing the operation and processes. How do things work? When one grows up in poverty, they have to learn how things work to fix it themselves by learning the operation and process because they cannot afford for someone to come and fix things for them. Same with the job or talent. We learn how our job operates and we learn the process until we no longer have to fake it. We become an expert and can teach it to the next person to fill our shoes. If you learn something, learn in a way to teach it to someone else, that is how you multiply. No matter what, we have to ask ourselves "what is success" to us. Then ask if it aligns with the plans of God. No matter what, even if you feel God is silent, keep developing yourself because God is answering.

Withdraw from dysfunctional people; they will hold you back from accomplishing God's will. Submitting to the order of our leadership or mentors, we learn and become fruitful and multiply. How we view our reality is tied to whom we are connected. Are the top five people on our go-to list people who have their life in order or building intentional actions to grow? Our connections become the makeup of what we attract. Distractions come to cause division with its key mission to get us to miss the mark when our focus is out of alignment.

Genesis 6:13-15

So God said to Noah, "I am going to put an end to all people, for the earth is filled with violence because of them. I am surely going to destroy both them and the earth. So make yourself an ark of cypress wood; make rooms in it and coat it with pitch inside and out.

This is how you are to build it...

Most people think of the story of Noah, God's voice as James Earl Jones or Morgan Freeman in the clouds saying in their deep booming eloquent voice, "If you build it, they will come," with thunder, lightning, and all that jazz. I'm pretty sure it was more subtle than that. God gave Noah a big dream to build an ark. It was kind of a strange vision because during that time rain had not existed, water came from the ground. Flooding had never occurred (vs 17). Here was a man who was faithfully obedient to the divine vision for 120 years (Genesis 6:3-7). God gave Noah the exact dimensions of the ark, what kind of wood, piece by piece design, and Noah completed the vision. God told Noah when to gather food, the animals, seven pairs of clean animals from every animal group and one pair of unclean animals from that animal group. They came two-by-two just like God said, and it took seven days to load the ark (Genesis 7). Dinosaurs did not make it on the ark. They died in the flood. God is always very detailed; He does not leave you guessing. Here is a man building something for an event that nobody in the world has ever heard of or seen, Noah kept the divine vision for 120 years. I am pretty sure people thought he was insane. For 120 years, Noah said yes to God and fulfilled the dream that God gave him. Not only that, but God also provided the resources. Then God also let Noah have dominion over the animals. Can you imagine the look on people's faces when all these animals lined up in their order? Noah says, "Okay, lions, now it's your turn to go into your section of the ark next to the lama." God's vision will give you order, details, dominion, resources and you execute the process.

Reap what you sow: sow seed for the dream, name your seed, call it good. Sow as you go, sow more after as a thank offering. What do you sow? Time, talent, and treasure. This is your investment in God's vision. It's an action that manifests God's promise to you.

Use your imagination

Jeremiah 24:3-4

Then the Lord asked me, "What do you see, Jeremiah?"

"Figs," I answered. "The good ones are very good, but the bad ones are so bad they cannot be eaten."

Then the word of the Lord came to me...

God pressed Jeremiah to see. God asked Jeremiah, "What do you see?" Once Jeremiah spoke the vision into existence, that was the action; then, God revealed His Word attached to the vision. In Jeremiah's case, it was a prophecy for the people of Israel. His vision was for a nation that was in captivity.

You need to surround yourself with BIG DREAMERS! Grow and build your faith with those who are like-minded in Christ. Make sure you do not share your dreams with people who are putting you down, agreeing with what is popular in the world that is not of the plan of God, or if they do not improve themselves in their own lives, they can misinterpret your vision and mess thing up. People who do not support themselves or support you will hinder and delay your assignment due to selfishness and their blindness to divine assignments and covenant. You are going to people for advice who have no spirit in them to carry your purpose, they will not once stop you and say, "Let's pray about this," and ask, "Is this what God wants?" If you choose to reject or mismanage what God asks you to do, God will find someone else to complete the task the way the vision was given, and you miss the blessing or reward attached to it. God needs a vessel to work and speak through. The person who says yes will get an even bigger reward and blessing because they faithfully chose what was God's desire. Keeping the right company keeps you in alignment with reaching your goal for the dream to come to pass. Ask God to show you the intent and hearts of people. He will show you whom to trust; it is most likely the people whom you least expect. Sometimes that means laying down your personal loyalties to people so you can do what God called you to do. Unfortunately, not everyone is going to like what God called you to if the call doesn't align with their selfish ambition, personal agendas, or a prideful image in their mind. If you do not know successful people, read books and watch documentaries on successful people. Stay close to someone who is doing what God wants you to do. Invest in the dream. Take your time with God to pray about how to invest in the dream. When God sees you investing in Him, that's when He provides for the vision. Be patient, investment and research take time.

"Slow success builds character. Rapid self-imposed success builds your ego."
- Bishop Dale Bronner

CHAPTER 7
PRAYER

Matthew 6:9-15 (NIV)

"This, then, is how you should pray:
"'Our Father in heaven,
hallowed be your name,
your kingdom come,
your will be done,
on earth as it is in heaven.
Give us today our daily bread.
And forgive us our debts,
as we also have forgiven our debtors.
And lead us not into temptation,
but deliver us from the evil one.'

For if you forgive other people when they sin against you, your heavenly Father will also forgive you. But if you do not forgive others their sins, your Father will not forgive your sins."

Even the disciples asked, "How do you pray?" Jesus gives an example of how and what to pray. Our prayers should be toward God and not toward us. Our focus should be a focus on the Kingdom of God in every situation. You can pray that way. Prayer is the greatest privilege. You should pray in times of happiness not just when you are in a bind. Most people reach out to God as a last resort going, "Oh, God help me!" In reality, you would not be begging God to help you if you hadn't prayed first. You have not because you ask not (James 4:2-3). First things first, we have to believe in God. We have to have faith in God who works all things out for our good. If we believe in God then we believe that He hears every prayer and petition, because He does. Every day is a new day. Each new day has new challenges and new blessings. Yesterday has gone; a second was a moment ago now that moment has gone. We need to pray each day for the new day and moment that is here right now. Ask God daily for His provision, to know His heart and mind because His grace and mercy are new every morning (Lamentations 3:22-23).

The outline of the Lord's Prayer is pretty clear and what to pray that addresses our past, present, and future. Prayer is not a session to vent and complain. Complaining is magnifying the situation. Faith is absent if we are only complaining instead of trusting God can turn our situation around. However, God does say "cast your burdens" on Him (1 Peter 5:7). If we are telling God our problems, make sure we acknowledge that God has the final say with the expectation that things will change with God's divine solution for your good. Understanding that all situations, even tragedies, are just a test for us to learn and grow in our character. Pray for the right direction because God is changing and challenging us to stretch our measure of faith for continual growth.

Prayer changes things: it changes one's heart, situations, even the course of nature that is aligned with His will that will bring Him eternal praise. The weapons we fight with are not weapons of this world; they are of the Kingdom of God. The authority over the enemy is by our words we speak from our mouth. The Bible says, "out of the abundance of our heart the mouth speaks" (Matthew 12:34). That means what our mouth speaks is what the heart is full of to create into being to speak blessings or cursing. Some people have to learn how to be happy. They must train their brains to think happy thoughts. If our hearts are full of turmoil, then we will speak turmoil. If our hearts are full of love, then we will speak compliments and joy. God says if we call on Him, He will answer (Psalm 91:15). One way to bring heaven down to earth is through prayer.

First, we have to stop talking about our problems and start magnifying and honoring God and His name. There is power in the name above every name, Jesus.

We start our prayer off with acknowledgment of the Lord. His dominion rules not just over our life but over everything; He is the Creator of the universe. This is where we meditate on the greatness and the magnitude of God. God is Almighty, Powerful, Awesome and Wondrous King of Glory, Holy (set apart), who is, was and is to come, always your Abba Father. Then, we praise God because He is faithful in love and mercy. Christ in us the hope of glory and on the throne in heaven. In us through the Holy Spirit that gives us access to God in heaven.

Pray God's will, not our will. Here is the heart of God. This is where we address anything and everything in our life that doesn't align with the heart of God. If it does not align with God's plan, His Word, and purpose, we are asking God to overrule our decisions. God's will be done. We believe it to be true on earth as it is in heaven. Now here are the personal petitions of daily provision. The first half of the Lord's prayer is about God and His Kingdom. The second half is about His purpose for us.

Daily bread is a reference to the Word of God. We need a word to align with our prayer. God's words and God's voice are speaking to us through the words written in the Bible. Our daily bread (word) is the provision and nourishment we need every day of our life. Jesus is the "Bread of Life" and "Living Water." These are the metaphors that Jesus used to explain spiritual nutrition for our day-to-day life. We partake in the Word of God daily, which means daily we invest in the Kingdom of God. This means being faithful in tithing, so God can supply our needs. Read the Word every day to provide the safety and provision not just to sustain our relationship with God but to sustain us in our daily challenges at home, on the job, in travel, or whatever it is we need for this day. We are daily prepared in all situations by the Word of God as our weapon in spiritual warfare.

1 John 1:9 (NIV)

If we confess our sins, he is faithful and just and will forgive us our sins and purify us from all unrighteousness.

If we were to translate this verse in the original text it would read *"If we say the same thing as God about our sins, God who exists is faithful and keeping the commands of God, forgive us our sins and cleanse us from all injustice; wrongfulness."*

Ask God to forgive us for not responding in a way that represents the Kingdom of God. There is a difference between saying "I'm sorry" rather than "forgive me." God is merciful to forgive. God is a loving God. Asking God to forgive us is not asking God to excuse our behavior. When one apologizes, they are speaking as if nothing happened. When someone asks for forgiveness, they are acknowledging that they have genuinely done something wrong. Confess our sins and repent (change our minds) to be in alignment with God. Daily we sin; we are all sinners. We either sin in action, verbally, or through our hearts or thoughts. Sin is being in rebellion and being in disobedience to God's Word and Kingdom principles that separate us from God. Ask God to forgive us, but also ask God for a new perception. For example, if I am hoping someone would fail, that is a sin. We should love our neighbors. We should confess our sin to God. Example: "God, I feel strong anger about this person." The next step is to ask God for a new perception, to see them as God sees them. It is those kinds of things that take time; it is a slow process. Lastly, we ask God to forgive us for feeling any way that opposes Christ, asking to show us God's way.

Matthew 6:14-15 (NIV)

For if you forgive other people when they sin against you, your heavenly Father will also forgive you. But if you do not forgive others their sins, your Father will not forgive your sins.

Pray for your enemies. Forgive them. This is addressing our heart and our maturity to handle persecution the right way. People will disappoint us. People will hurt us. People will do things that mismanaged the relationship somehow. A feud is an enmity, bitterness, grudges, or hostility between people. It happens for whatever reason. Every division has two sides of opinions. We have failed at some point in time as well. Do not gossip about your enemy. Pray to God for their heart as well as your own to forgive those who trespassed against you. Let God take care of their hearts as He is working on yours. As God forgives us, we forgive them, even if they do not ask for forgiveness. It is plain: if we do not forgive them, God will not forgive us. Again, this might take time, but set your pride aside. As we renew our hearts and minds, we are being transformed into God's image to not just love God but to love people.

Romans 12:20 (NKJV)

Therefore "If your enemy is hungry, feed him; If he is thirsty, give him a drink; For in so doing you will heap coals of fire on his head."

We need protection against the lies of the devil that makes us compromise God's will. Some things seem like a 'good' thing in a moment when it is happening, but it is not always the 'God' thing. If we are tempted, we will fail if we give into temptation. If we are tempted, we will not accomplish God's will to be done on earth as it is in heaven. Temptation always looks or seems good at the moment. Temptation distracts us from walking in God's purpose to please our fleshly desires. God is not going to bless our premarital sex. God is not going to bless our intoxication. God is not going to bless our gossip. God is not going to bless our thieving. Disobedience is a wicked spiral toward death.

What standard do we hold other Christians too? When we go into a church, we expect a pastor or leader in the church to behave a certain way all the time. We also should ask ourselves if we are holding ourselves to those same standards. The same mandate of the highest standard that is on the pastor to be a representative of God is the same mandate and highest standard God gave us to be separate from the world. Remember someone is always watching us. God is holding us accountable. The temptation is just ammo for the devil to say, "see this person is not saved, this person is not transformed." Those are lies. However, to permit bad behavior is to participate. It is better to pluck your eye out or chop your hand off than to give into temptation of sin (Matthew 18:8-9). Ask God to not let us fall into temptation. We ask for wisdom and to rid ourselves of foolishness that will lead us in the wrong direction. We have to give up things, sometimes people, that are tempting to ourselves, which will be different for everyone. Be diligent in turning away from whatever it is that can easily distract us away from Christlike conduct.

Ask boldly; ask in faith. Keep asking. Be persistent. Believe what we currently don't see. Believe and expect that God will answer and accomplish what we are asking in prayer.

1 Timothy 2:1 (NIV)

I urge, then, first of all, that petitions, prayers, intercession and thanksgiving be made for all people.

Tongues

When a person receives the baptism of the Holy Spirit the evidence is speaking in "tongues." "Tongues" is one of the gifts that the Holy Spirit imparted to believers as their prayer language individually or for the corporate body of believers in Christ. When we speak in "tongues," our prayer language is the Holy Ghost speaking mysteries up to the throne room of God on our or others' behalf. Tongues are what the spirit speaks, not what our flesh speaks. Interpretation of tongues comes when the mysteries need to be spoken to the corporate body of believers for divine understanding and knowledge when God is speaking supernaturally. Sometimes a person who speaks another language will hear the "tongues" spoken in their language with a word from that Lord specifically to that person when others did not hear a natural language spoken. Tongues are a sign for unbelievers and operate closely with the gift of prophecy and interpretation.

1 Corinthians 14:2, 27-30 (NIV)

For anyone who speaks in a tongue does not speak to people but to God. Indeed, no one understands them; they utter mysteries by the Spirit.

If anyone speaks in a tongue, two—or at the most three—should speak, one at a time, and someone must interpret. If there is no interpreter, the speaker should keep quiet in the church and speak to himself and to God.

Two or three prophets should speak, and the others should weigh carefully what is said. And if a revelation comes to someone who is sitting down, the first speaker should stop.

Getting alone with God

Getting alone with God is extremely important to do. Get a designated area that is special just you and God to study the Word and wait patiently to hear the Word of God speak when the word resonates in your spirit to come forth out of your mouth. Even a place where you can 'war' in prayer. It's called *tarrying*. If you can tarry in prayer for an hour you will see the travail of your soul with divine insight. The reason at least an hour is important because the number 60 in the Bible is a foundational number to uphold, help, or support; called *samekh* in Hebrew, the symbol looks like a shield or hedge. When we are in the glory presence of God, we lose the concept of time. "With the Lord a day is like a thousand years, and a thousand years are like a day" (2 Peter 3:8). Sometimes we must set our agenda aside and pray all night long till we feel the heaviness lift off our hearts.

Jesus always separated himself to get alone to pray, as it was his custom (Luke 22:39). Getting alone with God takes away the distractions of the world so we can hear the voice of God through the Holy scriptures. When we read the Word, we ask God to illuminate the words that are meant for us at that moment. Then we ask God to show us how to apply the Word to our lives. We pray for hours or longer in some cases. Not only are we building intimacy, but we are receiving insight and revelation from God about what we are praying for. Long prayers also allow the Holy Spirit to do His best work in us due to our submission.

Getting alone with God builds an intimate relationship with God where there are no boundaries. We come as we are, vulnerable, honest with hearts set to pray for change that aligns with God's will. This is the time to meditate on the Word of God and pray. Most of the Psalms were written in solitude with God by David ranging from worship to the deepest despair. We are safe in God's presence to express ourselves freely without judgment, holding nothing back from God. God takes what we have and shows us His way, His truth, and His life in every area to focus our alignment to His divine purpose designed for us.

2 Corinthians 1:20 (NIV)

For no matter how many promises God has made, they are "Yes" in Christ. And so, through him the "Amen" is spoken by us to the glory of God.

There is no "if" in God, only "yes" and "Amen." **Amen** means at the end - so it is, so be it, may it be fulfilled. It was a custom in the synagogues that when God's Word has spoken the utterance of the "Amen" was a declaration that the Word of God is an agreement that says yes, most certainly God's promise is for me. We hear God's Word. God is saying "yes" that word, that promise is for me because we feel the Holy Spirit stirring in our hearts, then we, in agreement with the Holy Spirit, say "Amen." When we pray don't pray "if" God will... pray "when" God will… It is believing the most definite answer. We must be very careful to not get discouraged, rush, or reject our answer when God's "yes" is not the image we had in our mind. His "yes" might be to humble our pride, open our eyes to new things, or shift our direction. It is still "yes," just not how we thought it would look in a different season.

Be consistent and in a place of prayer. If we do not know how to prepare for our visitation with God, start with an example of the story of the Shunammite woman in 2 Kings 4:8-37. She perceived that Elisha was a prophet of the Lord that was traveling with no place to stay. Understanding that being in close proximity to this man of God was going to bring great blessing and protection, even though she was of a different faith, she prepared a room for Elisha and opened her home completely to him because of the divine "anointing" or "mantel" that he carried. Just like the Shunammite woman who prepared for Elisha's visitation, prepare for God's visit this way in the chambers of your home:

1. **Room** - This is the place for God to freely dwell. Your prayer closet or 'war room'.
2. **Chair** - See it as the throne of God. Your prayers are the incense that goes up to the throne room of God.
3. **Table** - Where you have fellowship with God.
4. **Lamp** – Presence of God. The lamp to your feet and the light on your path.
5. **Cot/Bed** - a place of rest when you put all your cares in the hands of God. So be it, amen.

Lamentations 2:19

Arise, cry out in the night, as the watches of the night begin; pour out your heart like water in the presence of the Lord. Lift up your hands to him for the lives of your children, who faint from hunger at every street corner.

Watches - 4th watch prayer

Our normal times of the day are separated into four parts: morning, midday, evening, midnight. Biblically, the Roman military set a total of eight times for watchmen who stood on top of city walls to be on guard for approaching danger. This would be during what would be our evening to morning, designated "watch" hours: **1st** (6pm – 9pm); **2nd** (9pm – 12am); **3rd** (12am – 3am); **4th** (3am – 6am); **5th** (6am - 9am); **6th** (9am - 12pm); **7th** (12pm - 3pm); **8th** (3pm - 6pm). The best teaching on "watches" is from Archbishop Nicolas Duncan-Williams from Ghana book *Enforcing Prophetic Decrees*, volume 2.

I am not going to talk about all the watch hours. The 3rd watch and 4th watch are the ones that people, even non-Christians, are unintentionally familiar with. Most people do not talk about watch hours, but it is good to know and understand times and seasons, especially spiritual operation. This would be most significant if you are called to evangelism or are in missionary work because you have access to unknown territories to take dominion over areas. Some areas are only active at night. At some point, you walk right into spiritual operations as it is happening at these times. An evangelist or missionary will see spiritual operations where most people just have a sense of spiritual activity. Even demonic activity is subjected to God's time and God's authority. Remember you are in God's army of the Lord; our mandate is to be on guard of the enemy's activities and also aware of the manifestation or the fulfillment of God's plans. God sets times and seasons, even prayer times.

Third watch hours are from 12:00 am (midnight) - 3:00 am. During this time is the most spiritual activity. This is the time that Satanists and witches call the "witching hours." They do most of their demonic activity during this time. For the people of God who were in bondage, chains break, deliverance is released at this time.

The Apostle Paul and Silas were released from prison at midnight (Acts 16:25). God released the people of Israel from Egypt at this time (Exodus 12:31-37). Samson escaped from Gaza at midnight by pulling off the gates of the city and carrying city gate doors, posts, and bars out with him (Judges 16:3-4).

Fourth watch hours are from 3:00 am - 6:00 am. Prayer warriors or "watchmen" are called into prayer battle to intercede and tarry *(keep praying until something happens)* during this time. Freedom and foundational blessings are released during this time at the start of a new day. Enforce victory from the warfare that happened during the 3rd watch, battle strategies, and the time when the enemies have to flee because they cannot operate in the light as the sun rises.

Jacob saw angels ascending and descending from heaven and then wrestled an angel and demanded a blessing at the fourth watch (Genesis 28:12). Peter walked on water during the fourth watch hour (Matthew 14:25). Gideon's battle ended at the top of the fourth watch and the outcome was a victory for the nation (Judges 7:17–22).

If you are woken up at 3 am with a feeling of a heavy weight of urgency on your heart, it is a call for prayer that demands you to intercede on your behalf or on behalf of others. Ask the Holy Spirit to guide you. Keep praying until that urgency lifts off of your heart. Some people call prayer intercessors "storm watchers" – these are people who can sense that something is coming before it happens. Sometimes it is good and sometimes it is bad, but we just know that a storm is approaching. Prayer is warfare.

Matthew 5:44 (NIV)

But I tell you, love your enemies and pray for those who persecute you.

I had entered into a pruning season. During this time, God had to cut away at anything in my life that had codependent attachments. God was not letting anything influence me by distracting opinions that would prevent God's direction from coming to pass. I was on my way to greet a person I dearly cared for. The moment I got up close to this person, I supernaturally saw in an open vision appear the word being written out. "B.E.T.R.A.Y.A.L." appeared huge on this person's forehead like a neon light. I kept saying in my heart to the Lord, "No, who is going to betray this person?" I started looking around the room with urgency trying to sense someone was going to betray this person. God started to show me it was not someone else, it was a spirit operating within them to betray me. This person allowed the corruption of gossip to come out of their mouth and searched for an agreement with lies that hindered their heart that put a mark of attack against me. The poison of division allowed betrayal to operate in them with the intent to suppress, demean, discredit and block what God was trying to do in my life at that time. God allowed me to see and hear things in a spiritual realm that I did not want to believe. The insight, revelation, discernment of spiritual warning was all new for me. I did not like it. This was my first open vision that God showed me while I was awake. Usually, I received a vision through dreams. God also allowed me to hear misleading conversations of the alliance of slander against me in rooms I was not in and plots of actions against me with wicked laughter before they happened. It was like putting a movie on fast forward. When you are grounded in the Holy Ghost, He gives you words of warning for your protection.

Jeremiah 11:18 (NIV)

Because the LORD revealed their plot to me, I knew it, for at that time he showed me what they were doing. But I was like a gentle and tame lamb brought to the slaughter; And I did not know that they had devised plots and schemes against me, saying, "Let us destroy the tree with its fruit; Let us cut him off from the land of the living, That his name be remembered no longer."

The spirit that was operating in this person's actions had revealed its name: the spirit of betrayal. I was in such shock that this person was my Judas. (Judas was one of the original twelve disciples who betrayed Jesus right before His crucifixion.) I thought I was going crazy; the revelation was a lot to handle in a crowded room. As I was standing in front of them, I felt a gentle hand on my shoulder as if holding me back. I heard the whispered words, "Stay calm, be still, just pray." I took a step back and waved bye. My heart was so heavy that I was nauseous. I went home that night and prayed like crazy, "Lord show me Your glory, show me Your truth." My intercession prayer was that of Jesus, "Lord, forgive them for they know not what they do" (Luke 23:34). "Lord, reveal to me my part; forgive me if I did anything wrong." Even though I knew bits and pieces of God's warning, I didn't know the deeper roots of a foul familiar spirit that was behind it. God showed me how to fight my battles with the Word of God. I pulled out anointing oil, started praying in the spirit, and coming against the evil spirit that had revealed its name that was operating for the assassination of my name and this friendship that was originally intended to be a powerful Kingdom covenant that was corrupted by a pattern of 'Jezebelic' behavior.

Psalm 116:4 (BSB)

Then I called on the name of the LORD: "O LORD, deliver my soul!"

We can't have sunshine without the rain. Seasons have a time limit. In certain seasons we must hunker down, getting in the Word of God until the storm passes. Seeing this affliction as a good thing, it was teaching me things (Psalm 119:71). I recognized immediately it was a test, and I wanted to pass the test so badly (Acts 17:11). During the test, God was teaching me lessons about my heart and most importantly about Him. Even though I was angry, God said, "I love them just as much as I love you; pray for their heart." Not only was I being stretched, but the Lord was helping me to trust the process despite affliction, urgently praying for the lost and their souls.

Psalm 138:3 (NASB)

On the day I called, You answered me; You made me bold with strength in my soul.

God had to put me in a solitary place under weighty pressure to teach me to be an intercessor, prayer warrior. That was the first time God called me to intercede on behalf of someone with urgency. I prayed for the posture of their heart and my heart in this trial facing the effects of devastation. I asked God if He would immediately convict me to repent so that my heart, my words, and actions would stay clean before God. It took everything in me to not fight back in the flesh, to keep speaking blessings out of my pain but fight supernaturally with the strength to stay calm although my heart was broken and hurting. God helped me to pass through that season safely. I learned God is always ahead of the devil on everything. God sustains us through it all; we are to thank God through hardship and the lessons we learn in the storms of life. Staying loving, patient, forgiving, and kind through to the very end, no matter what. This might sound weird, but I thank God He allowed that person to betray me. If it had been someone else, I would not have cared enough to submit under God's authority to learn the lessons and discover supernatural gifts and revelations if someone else was being pruned from me. The betrayal had a purpose, and that purpose was a blessing.

Hebrews 11:1

Now faith is confidence in what we hope for
and assurance about what we do not see.

People around a good intercessor might think something is always wrong with them. That is not true; the intercessor is just called to pray. The intercessor is gifted to carry the weight of a heavy burden and they know they must get alone with God to pray the burden up into the courtrooms of heaven until the burden lifts. When we accept the call to watch and pray, we pray without ceasing and will not faint. We must persistently pray boldly with authority to deploy angelic assistance who war on our behalf. As an intercessor of prayer will strategically pray for people, locations, regions, and national revival and growth in those areas. Prayer intercessors know how to war in the spiritual realms, exposing hidden things in the dark places and calling them into the light. The intercessor feels the need to call to repentance and be revived to a new life in Christ Jesus. Our prayers on the power of God to bring blessings to us from all over the place. A prayer warrior faces a lot of spiritual warfare because their prayers have the power to break bondages standing in the gap between the issues and God. Through prayer and intercession, God will allow doors to open where our name is being spoken and people find us, bring contracts to increase our portion, and give us influence. Prayer is the key that calls things into being by faith.

Romans 8:34 (NIV)

Who then is the one who condemns? No one. Christ Jesus who died—more than that, who was raised to life—is at the right hand of God and is also interceding for us.

No matter the season, joyous times, or struggles, Jesus is interceding for us. Jesus Christ, the Righteous One, who sits on the throne at the right hand of God is our Advocate with the Father (1 John 2:1). The Lord is our light and salvation. We shall not fear but we will wait on Jesus and put our trust in Jesus that He is working all things out for our good. We will remain confident that we will see the goodness of the Lord in all our circumstances (Psalm 27). We place our hope in God during our waiting while we continually pray to God. We know and are confident that Jesus is speaking to the Father on our behalf, sending angels to minister to us with special graces along the way as signs that we are close to our victory. This is not the time to waver. The Lord wants us to talk to God about everything, be specific about everything. Talk to God about your family, job, your health, your food in your refrigerator. Prayer will change things; God will supply all your needs. Do not worry about anything but pray about everything (Philippians 4:6-7). Cast your anxieties on God, unload and receive a refreshing from God. His mercies are new every morning. God will take responsibility to take our battles and our prayers if we seek first the Kingdom of God. We believe God no matter what circumstances look like or what was said, God has the final say. We keep our hope and trust in Jesus the Hope of Glory to come through at the right time. We rely on the Holy Spirit to help us endure with great strength through the joy of the Lord. The Lord is our shepherd. He is in control. Everything has to submit and bow at the name of Jesus; demons have to flee. As we call on His great name, we know Jesus is our great intercessor advocating on our behalf to God for our victory.

Hebrews 7:25 (NIV)

Therefore he is able to save completely those who come to God through him, because he always lives to intercede for them.

CHAPTER 8
ASK GOD

John 14:6–7 (NIV)

Jesus told him, "I am the way, the truth, and the life. No one comes to the Father except through me. If you know me, you will also know my Father. From now on you do know him and have seen him."

Prayer changes a multitude of things, but we need to know what to ask God for. Sure, it seems easy to ask for luxurious things. Remember God is not prideful and does not care for the things we desire that are in vain. However, God will supply our needs sometimes even before we ask and, in our obedience, to first seeking the Kingdom of God. We receive rewards that are our hearts' desires. We heard that Jesus said, "ask and we receive," but then it seems like the things that we are praying for either don't happen, don't happen quickly enough, or don't happen in the way that we had hoped. We end up questioning, did God hear us? Jesus sits at the right hand of the Father in heaven to intercede on our behalf. When Jesus died on the cross at Calvary, the veil that separated us from communicating personally with God was torn. We are now able to come to God in the name of Jesus and ask God for whatever we want ***IF*** it is according to His will. What does that mean?

In the Old Testament, the Israelites had the Ark of the Covenant. Covenant means a legal contract of agreement. This is the promise of God that He will be our God, we are His people. It was conditional. Keep His laws and statutes and God will keep His promise of blessings and provisions. The place where God would dwell was in the place called the Holies of Holies. It was the most sacred place. God's glory dwelt there. God's presence sat on the Ark of the Covenant behind a huge veil. Only the priest could enter into this area to be face to face with God. The priests wore bells on the bottom of their garments for people on the other side of the veil would know they were still alive. Anyone else who was not the priest that came face to face with God in the natural would die. When Jesus died on the cross at Calvary, the veil in the Temple that separated everyone from coming to God on their own was torn from top to bottom. Now we have access to God through the Holy Spirit. God no longer dwells in the Temple behind a veil. When you accepted Jesus, you gave access for the Holy Spirit to come upon you. The Holy Spirit lives in you, now you are the temple of God. You have access to God because His Spirit is in you. You communicate with God, the Holy Spirit, in the name of Jesus through the posture of your heart.

God is not Santa Claus, the Easter Bunny, or a gene in a bottle. There is no witchcraft here or lies of deception to get what you want out of God. God is conditional, and it is according to His will and the Kingdom of Heaven's plan that God set for you before you were formed in your mother's womb. We do not ask God to tell us the numbers for the lottery because God does not do that. If we ask God, in Jesus's name, according to His will x, y, and z will happen, and we will be abundantly blessed. What are *x, y, and z*? Read the Bible and God will reveal mysteries to you through His Word that *x, y, and z* are for you. God says, "For I know the **plans I have for you**," declares the Lord, "plans to **prosper** you and not to harm you, plans to give you **hope** and a **future**" (Jeremiah 29:11). These are God's plans, not our plans. What is for us, is for us alone and not for someone else, although it will bless people connected to us. As much as someone might want to claim your revelation, or not accept it, the revelation is between you and God. That revelation or vision is for us to be God's vessel in this world to follow Kingdom order and become fruitful and multiply, whether God called us to the office of ministry or to be the mailman. We are designed for Kingdom business no matter where we are. When we ask God for anything; first things first, does this align with God's heart, and is this according to His will for our lives? Am I producing the fruits of the Holy Spirit that reflects unity or am I producing fruits of an evil spirit that are producing division? This is another way that we are honoring God by addressing what He wants first above our personal desires.

Matthew 15:11 (NIV)

"What goes into someone's mouth does not defile them, but what comes out of their mouth, that is what defiles them."

What you speak will manifest, come to pass. You hear people say, "be careful what you say," and there is truth to that. The world was created when God commanded the world into existence when He spoke. In the beginning, God created the heavens and the earth. "Now the earth was formless and empty, darkness was over the surface of the deep, and the **Spirit of God was <u>hovering</u> over the waters**. ***<u>God said</u>***, 'Let there be light,' and **there was light**. God saw that the light was good, and he separated the light from the darkness. **<u>God called</u>** the light 'day,' and the darkness he called 'night.' And there was evening, and there was morning—the first day" (Genesis 1:1-5). It is the same when you ask God. You are speaking to God about what you want to happen. The words of God's mouth were like the wind flowing through the atmosphere to activate the Holy Spirit that was hovering over the waters. Once God spoke a command, that activated the request in action. When you speak a thing, that word spoken activates the manifestation of the request given to call things into existence. We are what we think, so when we grumble out of our hearts and say, "I'm broke," or, "I'm ugly," or other curses of lies unto ourselves. We are calling those things into existence. When you speak, "I'm happy, I'm rich," those are the things you are calling into existence. Your words have power to create a thing. You may be creating an atmosphere that defiles you or others. Change the words that come out of your mouth.

Proverbs 18:21

The tongue has the power of life and death,
and those who love it will eat its fruit.

A great forest can be set on fire by one tiny spark. The words you speak are a spark that starts the flame of fire. God hears what we say every day, if we talk good or bad. Even when words not spoken, God searches the heart to find out what we really feel. If you sow disrespect, you reap disrespect. If you sow love, you reap love. Your words will ignite the fire of blessing or cursing. The words you speak are the command you call into existence. You have an opportunity to ignite the fire of Jesus when things are darkest in your life. Jesus is the fire that dispels all darkness.

Matthew 7:7-8 (NIV)

Ask and it will be given to you; seek and you will find; knock and the door will be opened to you. For everyone who asks receives; the one who seeks finds; and to the one who knocks, the door will be opened.

When we believe salvation is by Jesus's death on the cross and His resurrection, our faith builds stronger in the trustworthy fact that we believe we are sanctified by faith, we believe we are justified by faith, we believe we are healed by faith. Faith is the assurance of things hoped for. That means we trust that God will do everything He said He would do according to His Word. Faith is a conviction of things not seen with the natural eye. Faith is believing God will work on your behalf. You expect miracles through faith.

Your hope in God is taking His Word seriously through your faith in Him who has your soul in His hands the moment you accept Jesus as your Lord and Savior. If you did not take God seriously or His Word seriously, then you would be ignoring or rejecting the promise of eternal reward. When you ignore or reject something, you are turning your back to that thing, which is an act of disrespect. You cannot take the Word of God seriously without respecting it, not just accepting comfort scriptures. "My soul is eternally saved. God supplies all my needs and protects me from storms." But when the Word of God convicts your heart that points out your sins, like hating or humiliating your neighbor or living a lifestyle that is perverted in God's eyes. God is asking us by our faith to not just accept the easy things but to change our ways and try some new, uncomfortable things that glorify God. We should not turn our back in disrespect saying I'll accept this but not that. God does not say to pick and choose what commands to follow or believe. God says those that follow all of what He had commanded (Deuteronomy 26:18) and those that will believe will receive treasures, blessings, and rewards. God wants you to take it all and wants to work with you in a partnership on the areas of conviction. God loves you where you are right now. God wants to help you even in the things that might seem or feel ugly.

When God says "ask in my name and I will do..." that was a promise to the disciples who gave up everything to follow Jesus. They were completely committed. They also had to learn how to accept and apply a new way of thinking and living. What Jesus was teaching was never done before; at that time, Jesus was revolutionary. The things people asked were not selfish requests. You have to ask yourself and reflect on your heart posture if your requests are selfish and temporary. People pray to God and ask God for a temporary moment when they are in the worst situation and then forget about God when everything is going well. Remember that Jesus was a teacher, too. He wants you to ask Him of things to learn. "Father, how do I become a good steward of my finances? Will you show me how?" "Father, how do I let go of toxic people in my life?" "Father, how do I apply your teachings to my life? Will you guide my steps?" "Father, will you give me strategies to be the problem solver on my job?" These questions are not temporary; they are eternal questions to learn a new way.

James 4:2-3 (AMP)

You are jealous and covet [what others have] and your lust goes unfulfilled; so you murder [extreme hatred in your heart]. You are envious and cannot obtain [the object of your envy]; so you fight and battle.

You do not have because you do not ask [it of God]. You ask [God for something] and do not receive it, because you ask with wrong motives [out of selfishness or with an unrighteous agenda], so that [when you get what you want] you may spend it on your [self-indulgent] desires.

Pursuit is the proof of your desire. Your destiny is inevitable and will chase you down and find you. Saul desired to kill all the Christians and stop them in their tracks. Destiny (Jesus) stopped Saul on the road to Damascus, changed his name from Saul to Paul, and made him one of the most influential evangelists for the Kingdom of God. His destiny was written in the majority of the New Testament (Acts 9). His desire to murder ended, and his destiny was to save souls for the Kingdom of God. God wants us to pursue the path of our destiny in Him.

A good thing is temporal, and a God thing is eternal. A good thing comes extremely easily. There is no effort because most of the good things are easy to say, "I did this or that," and it is almost too good to be true. Good things disguise themselves as "God" things, but at some point, the veil comes off and it leads you in the wrong direction. Saul thought he was doing justice by killing Christians and stopping the Gospel from being spread across the world. He was headed in the wrong direction that he thought was a good thing until Jesus stopped him in his tracks. "No, you are not going to kill my people, you are my guy to preach the Gospel." When he went out to start preaching the Gospel and not killing Christians, that was the God thing. People were scared of him, they didn't believe he changed, and he suffered in many ways. But the reward of the fruits is eternally written in the majority of the New Testament.

God will give you a vision. Most likely it is the end result of the vision. Then you realize as you go through what it will cost you to accomplish the vision. When it is God, your flesh will always want to resist it. You feel like you are unqualified, unprepared, or it is not the right time. There are never enough resources to back it up. I heard it once said, "God never gives you a dream that matches your budget. God never checks your bank account or asks anyone for permission. God checks your faith." There may be no money, no people around to help or agree, nothing. There is opposition on every side. Why? So that God gets all the glory, you get the benefit. The enemy doesn't like that. Individuals will try to belittle you or talk you out of what God called you to do. This is where you draw the line in the sand. Either you choose the God thing that might be hard, unpopular, and uncomfortable at first or the good thing that is easy, popular, and comfortable. That is why you cannot tell everyone what God shared with you. You must protect the God thing. No accomplishment of eternal value in God's Kingdom is a result of men's efforts. When you are at your weakest, your dependence relies on God that is when you can do all things through Christ. God gets the glory in it. You get the eternal reward and the benefits of favor because you allowed God to use you as a vessel. It was not you; it was God. You cannot take the credit. God gets the glory.

The moment we start to compare is the moment we step out of God's will. A comparison is a form of vanity. Not everything is social media worthy. Your blessing is God-worthy. The question is, do we fear God, or do we fear people? Stepping away from the popularity, for those who understand our revolutionary purpose will support us. Our expression should be what matters to God and His image not what matters to people and their image. Bishop Dale Bronner said, "Slow blessing builds your character and rapid blessings build your ego." God showed us in private revelations the value, time, dedication, and how to honor the answer and the delicate preciousness of the integrity of the assignment or answered prayer. The blessing we prayed for does not always come already packaged. It does not look like the image in our mind because it was the end result. God showed us what we have to discover in the blessing, then build with limited resources God gave us the trial to bring out the best of this responsibility to stretch our faith. Someone who did not receive this revelation is not going to agree nor understand the level of importance to what God said, they might oppose it completely. Or they might believe what God showed you so much that out of envy they plot sabotage against your call and connections by slandering your name in both public and private. They do not want to see you blessed more than them and your desires to come to pass, so they will do everything they can to block your progress. They might even try to steal your blessing and call it their own. But God is a vindicator.

The test comes when those that are close to us dangle a carrot of opportunity in front of our faces that look easy and feels better all around, but it opposes what God showed us in private. God gives us the free will to choose a window of opportunity to come into agreement with one or the other. Either we accept what He has for us, shake hands with God's truth and say yes, or we shake hands in agreement with easy comfort and reject the truth. Once that window of blessings passes, the opportunity is over, and God has to keep going. Once God starts something, it does not stop. God is eternal. So, either God has to find someone else to obey and reap the reward or continue the plan with you and you receive the blessing. If we missed this opportunity, God will give us another opportunity with something else that will help us learn to choose God first. That is why some situations feel like we pressed the repeat button. We missed the exam now we have to take the test all over again.

The only time God will intervene and tell you "no" to the vision He gave you that was originally a "yes" is if you are operating in destructive behavior for yourself or toward the assignment. God must protect what He ordained. God did that with Adam. Two trees in the Garden were to be respected, Tree of the Knowledge of good and evil and the Tree of Life. Adam ate from the Tree of Knowledge and God blocked Adam from the Tree of Life to protect Adam and the tree from eternal sin (Genesis 3). That is why Jesus paid the price for eternal salvation (John 19:28-30).

When God told Noah about the flood, the ark did not appear out of thin air. Noah had to build the boat. That means Noah had to cut down trees, carve out the wood, and follow the plan of God for 120 years. Noah had to be willing to be humiliated and subject to ridicule because no one had ever seen rain before this. Once 120 years ended, all production for this skyscraper of a boat had to stop and the rain came. Why this obedience? Because Noah loved God and trusted God's word no matter what other people said. All Noah did was say yes to God (Genesis 6–9).

You will go through these tests of faith. God will propose something to you that is revolutionary and unusual because it was never done before. It is our choice to follow Jesus or not. It is a test of trust and faith. You choose to trust and respect what God gave you. You either invest in the assignment or you choose to doubt and disrespect the assignment. You reject it. Every time you say yes to Jesus, you must learn everything God's way. You must learn how to manage what God is giving you. If your assignment is a person or a new location or whatever is of God, when you agree with God, God will give you something unique and revolutionary to fulfill it. You have to learn everything God's way. The new way will get you completely out of your comfort zone. Your choice is to agree with God's way or agree with your way. There is power in agreement, God's power or man's power. You have to ask God all the right questions. God will give you supernatural power to accomplish the assignment with excellence. He said, "Ask and I will give to you," "Ask and I will show you." "You have not because you ask not" sometimes you are asking the wrong questions. No, God is not going to give you the lottery numbers to get rich quick; that is man's way. Yes, God will show you how to steward your finances to get you out of debt. God's way is tithing your first fruits.

Asking God the right questions to help you through is vitally important toward your journey. Faith and trust go hand in hand. God will open many doors of opportunities to walk in. God also gives you the power to choose. The main question to ask God is "Is this your will and purpose for my life?" That is always number one. During times of testing and training, it might feel like boot camp. God will help you. Asking God for help in every step is the perfect question. If you need wisdom, God will give you wisdom. If you need food, God will provide nourishment. If you need finances, God will help you get the money. If you need a mentor or a friend, God will send you a friend. All of this takes time. If you need help being patient, God will help you with that, too. The moment you try to do it yourself or feel like you know what is best, you have hardened your heart to God's instructions and that is an action of disrespect because you are rejecting the God thing for the "good" thing. Ask God to take the veil off of your eyes, unplug your ears, and keep your heart postured toward God. God is showing you new things. Learn a new way. Ask your teacher, Jesus, every question possible to complete the assignments He gives you. You will discover so many hidden treasures when you say yes to the God thing. God will answer every question to help you along the way when you ask according to His will with the right motives.

Proverbs 19:21 (AMP)

Many plans are in a man's mind,
But it is the Lord's purpose for him that will stand (be carried out).

CHAPTER 9
BREAKING CHAINS

Luke 22:31-32 (NIV)

"Simon, Simon, Satan has asked to sift all of you as wheat. But I have prayed for you, Simon, that your faith may not fail."

It seems strange that when we come to Christ, we think everything will be perfect and our expectations are immediate blessing and change. Well, for some people they get immediate favor and blessings, there are immediate changes, and you know it is from God. However, for some, the moment they step into the alignment of their God-given path, everything goes crazy. I see it as a two-way part that goes hand in hand. God makes trials work together for our good. First, trials come to test our faith that produces perseverance to lead us to maturity in Christ (James 1:2-4). Other trials the devil lies to make us believe we are not free in Christ and think of our lives as filled with hardship. The devil will do everything he can to keep our thoughts bound in lies, assumptions, and mischief. The chains of our thoughts come to destroy our future, limit our potential, and paralyze our hope to move forward, putting us into a vicious cycle of dysfunction that affects our circumstances around us. The adversary only fights with people he is intimidated with because anyone who carries the weight of God's glory as a child of God attracts the attacks of the opposition. The truth is, we are set free from bondage by the blood of Jesus, and the devil does not know the truth that we are no longer in bondage. The devil is a liar and ALWAYS (John 8:44) operates in deceit and manipulation. The devil's mission is to steal, kill, and destroy (John 10:10), in that order. It is always in three ways as the "lust of eyes" (materialism), "lust of body / flesh" (hedonism), and "pride of life" (egoism) (1 John 2:16). Just like the Holy Spirit needs a vessel to operate in Kingdom business, so does any evil spirit need a vessel to stop Kingdom business from happening. Unfortunately, I have found that these tests and trials are usually with the people who are closest to me.

When Jesus received the Holy Spirit and fire (Matthew 3:11), He went into the wilderness to be alone, fast, and pray for 40 days. At the end of 40 days, the devil came to tempt Jesus in three ways: 1) turning a stone into bread to satisfy His hunger by performing a magic trick, 2) to throw Himself off a cliff so angels can catch Him for a public spectacle, then 3) lastly to worship Satan for the kingdoms of the world. In every temptation, Jesus spoke the Word of God against every lie and overcame the temptations by the Word of God. The devil left Jesus because Jesus did not sin, and the reward was the power of the Holy Ghost (Luke 4:1-14). Then Jesus began His ministry. You can fight the devil with the Word of God to defeat all the things coming against you. Read the Word of God to know the Word of God. That is why it is so important to read your Bible.

Sometimes early sufferings prove for the best. Trial, persecution, rejection, and all kinds of sufferings teach us to pray with urgency. Early suffering leads to an early awareness that weans us from the world and turns our attention away from our sinful nature. Without suffering, we would never discover that God is a deliverer to those who love Him. Know that suffering is only for a season. It is a season of circumcision or pruning (to cut things off). To take the weeds of our life, finding the source to uproot the problem and rid ourselves of things that are not fruitful. Lastly, it is a change of direction. That change forces us to have full reliance on God alone. Change is uncomfortable because we lose control and trust God for the next move, which becomes a fear of the unknown.

James 1:2-4

Consider it pure joy, my brothers and sisters, whenever you face trials of many kinds, because you know that the testing of your faith produces perseverance. Let perseverance finish its work so that you may be mature and complete, not lacking anything.

I saw a meme that said, "You cannot detox an entire decade in a day." Everything takes time. The testing that we go through takes time. We pass through the trial not stopping but keep going. Some people settle in a place that is almost enough. Almost is not good enough. People sometimes become emotionally bound when relationships end and have a hard time moving forward with their lives. Others become mentally bound when they suffer some sort of tragedy and get stuck in that place constantly talking about what happened twenty years ago. These tests of life are not supposed to keep us in chains. You have to believe that the chains are loosed.

1 Peter 1:6-7 (NRSV)

"In this you rejoice, even if now for a little while you have had to suffer various trials, so that the genuineness of your faith — being more precious than gold that, though perishable, is tested by fire — may be found to result in praise and glory and honor when Jesus Christ is revealed."

Some tests are short, and some tests take years to pass through. Each test has an end date. There are some tests that God allows that seem repeated until you ask God, "Okay, Lord, show me what it is I need to learn and help me pass through this test victorious." Otherwise, we will always think the adversary uses the same tactics over and over. Do not give the adversary so much credit. Sometimes it is our bad choices or bad behaviors we were taught that God is trying to undo.

Haven't you ever noticed some repeated cycles that happen in your life? You keep dating the same type of person. Certain incidents keep happening over again. It's like never-ending déjà vu. That can happen generationally, too. Your grandfather was one way, your father became the same way, and so on. Some people call it a familiar spirit repeating the cycle. Others called it a generational curse. Some people call it soul-ties that have not been broken. Sometimes ungodly spirits can transfer and attach themselves to you through your connections by some sort of sin or disobedience causing a breach in your spiritual hedge of protection. Addictions, bad relationships we cannot let go of, and the weird changes in our behaviors that were affected by our associations. We have to be careful about whom we are connected to, including our family, what we watch, what we listen to, what we read, and what we allow and the spirit behind those things can open the door to ungodly spirits to run wild in our life, in our home, in our family. For example, every parent knows whom their child should and should not hang around. When their child gets around a certain friend who is a liar and a thief, that kid influences their child to act and talk differently, doing things that are out of their character. As parents, we have two choices, either continue to let our child be wrongly influenced or cut off that friendship completely and get our child out of that environment with no access to this person again. There are people and things in our lives that we see every day which influence us positively or negatively.

A family can experience multiplications of bad habits, behavioral patterns, addictions, or perversion. These are learned behaviors that turn into repeated cycles. If you feel there is a demonic spirit that followed your bloodline for years, I have good news for you. The blood of Jesus broke any and all curses and covered your sin when He shed His blood on the cross of Calvary (Galatians 3:13). Christ redeemed us from the curse of the law by becoming a curse for us, for it is written, "Cursed is everyone who is hung on a pole." The moment you accepted Jesus as your Lord and Savior, then submitted every area of your life to be under the blood of Jesus, any and all curses were broken off of you, your children, and their children. Now all you have to do is step out of the cycle of bad behaviors. Do not repeat any of those dysfunctional behaviors, stop talking to the same people, and speak against every negative thing that has tormented you and your family for years. If you were born into domestic violence, you do not have to accept that as your fate. Rebuke every form of abuse that comes against you because you have authority in Jesus to command it to go. In the ***name*** of Jesus, every demonic attack has to flee. **Keep speaking the name of Jesus because there is power in the <u>name</u> and the <u>blood</u> of Jesus to set you free.** God is using you to be a barrier breaker for you and your family from the moment you accepted Jesus as your Lord and Savior. It stops with you. That behavior, addiction, and sickness have to go. You are armed and dangerous in the Holy Ghost. Release yourself, your mind, heart, and actions from falling into the patterns that keep this cycle alive. This is when you have to say to yourself and any spirit operating against you, "I have accepted Jesus as my Lord and Savior, the devil no longer has authority to distract me with false teachings, the cycle stops today. This will no longer affect me or my children. I am setting my mind on Christ and letting the Holy Spirit transform me into the person He has called me to be." Jesus's blood redeemed you, and that means you are free. You can freely walk in your authority to overcome cycles and behaviors that are no longer a part of you.

2 Corinthians 10:3-4 (NIV)

For though we live in the world, we do not wage war as the world does. The weapons we fight with are ***not*** *the weapons of the world. On the contrary, they have divine power to demolish strongholds."*

The war and battle we live in are the distractions that alter our perception. The adversary comes after us in three ways of diversion that cause division: noise, hurry, and crowds. Each is a set to block or hinder us from fulfilling God's purpose. The enemy sees our greatness before we know how great we are. Remember the bigger the attack, the bigger the blessing. If the attacks are in public so everyone can see, the blessing will be bigger in public so that our enemies can see how great God is in our life. God will vindicate us mightily. Do not fear; be strong and courageous (Joshua 1:9). Most importantly, we must set our minds on Christ. It is okay to be emotional. We are humans with feelings; it is natural. Do not let our emotions override our ability to stand firm on God's Word, taking control of our thoughts and who we are in Christ. There are snakes in the gardens of our minds; we need to know where those distractions are.

Noise: The adversary is always loud and projects itself to overshadow the still small voice. People who operate in pride or desire to be on top or attention-seeking always seem to be the loudest in the room. When you confront them, they usually let you speak first to build up a baseline for attacks to get you off guard. They answer raising their voice during discussions as a form of aggressive manipulation. This comes with judgment and criticism, negative surprises, and negative humor that belittles a person to make the adversary look superior. The adversary will operate in overconsumption that overwhelms an individual with intellectual bullying. The adversary's mission is to block the individual and make their life more difficult, point out weaknesses or flaws, and overshadow their intelligence, waiting for their next move to generate surprise attacks, not giving them time or space to answer or defend themselves. Even the atmosphere can be loud. You walk into a room and you sense so much tension. The noise will drown out peace and is intended to make sure you are not heard or able to speak.

Hurry: The rush drowns out patience and makes us exhausted by keeping us busy. God is still, calm, and peaceful. Satan rushes, is anxious, and impatient. The enemy tries to make things happen before its ordained time. The devil gives a false urgency of excessive indulgence of needing more and sets situations out of order to confuse. The enemy tries to force you into situations that make you lose your control and composure to open you up for attacks verbally or physically to slander your character. Sometimes you are promised something. At the proper time, it will be given to you. The devil will lie and say that the time is now when it is out of order, prematurely entering into a position or situation that you arrived too soon or not supposed to be in at all. Situations that should have been are not going in your favor because it is out of order. Premature death, rape, panic attacks, gluttony, and chaos are derivatives of this tactic. This is the devil's tactic to disrespect God's time, order, and seasons.

Crowds: The enemy always has a sidekick. Where there is one demon, there are many. God can be everywhere and anywhere at the same time. The devil cannot. The devil is only authorized to be in one place at a time. What the devil does is gather demonic forces that do his dirty work. The devil will assign legions of demons to bind people with all kinds of perversions. For example, he will start with the biggest meddling gossiper you know to stir the pot who operates in the spirit of jealousy, envy, pride, and insecurity. Those who eat their words will enjoy it (Proverbs

18:21). This group will go out of their way to research and pay close attention to your actions for evidence; this is a form of a spirit of idolatry. Since the devil is arrogant, he wants an audience, for example, those passive-aggressive social media messages that people post intended for certain people. Since they cannot say it to their face and because the enemy cannot operate alone, they are looking for an audience to be in agreement; 50 "likes" of the spirit of pettiness. The plot against someone is always dirty and messy. The adversary gathers people together who allow hate to operate in their hearts to shake hands in agreement to plot attacks, schemes, traps, and deception as a group against the individual. Throughout history, there has always been a mob formed against a revolutionary. The adversary does not know how to operate alone; it needs an alliance. If it operated alone, the adversary would always be defeated. The adversary will get back up, rallying groups of people together to form a mob to gang together to hate one person and call it 'loyalty' when it should be called 'codependency'.

Acts 3:15 (ISV)

you killed the source of life, whom God raised from the dead. We are witnesses to that.

Be very careful not to entertain these kinds of behaviors or join in on the mob mentality. You should not hate someone because someone else hates them. You are not called to fight someone else's battle. Just because someone got mad at another person does not mean others need to be mad at them, too. If we shake hands with someone who plays a victim and rallies people against an individual, we might lose out on a great blessing from that person they are plotting against who was sent to bless and help. Be careful not to hurt the one that God sent to help. It is very dangerous to sow seeds of dishonor and disrespect because that is what you will reap thirty, sixty, or a hundred-fold. If you slander someone's name, expect to be slandered, unless you repent. Sometimes the

Holy Spirit will convict your heart so that you will have to apologize for your dishonor and disrespect, not a meme on social media for yourself loathing attention because you are too prideful to apologize to their face or pick up the phone to have a mature conversation. God instructs us to pay what we owe them, if honor - give honor, if respect - give respect (Romans 13:7). Do not withhold good from those who deserve it, when it is within your power to act (Proverbs 3:27). The enemy is a coward that would rather keep the division because they're too arrogant to admit they're wrong. God will always try to reconcile for unity and peace (Matthew 5:24, Romans 12:18).

Isaiah 58:11 (NRSV)

"The LORD will guide you continually, and satisfy your needs in parched places, and make your bones strong; and you shall be like a watered garden, like a spring of water, whose waters never fail."

People always have lots to say about lives they never lived. As we can see, we have all sinned and fallen short in one way or another into these tactics, we were either the attacker or the victim (Romans 3:23). Remember the enemy wants to drown us out completely as if we never existed. The enemy sees us as a threat. Anytime we make progress, the enemy comes in one of these ways to block our progress. The devil will use people and situations to try to take us out. God will always have a way to make His plans through us succeed despite what is going on around us. God keeps us safe and protected even though things happen that try to stop us. We have the authority in the name of Jesus to pull down strongholds and get the devil under our feet (1 Corinthians 10:4-5). We have the authority over every evil spirit operating in cycles, overbearing plots causing misalignment in our lives. We have to get our minds off of these negative things and keep our focus on Jesus. Our perception is what leads us toward victory. Anything distorting our perception has to go.

God placed a hedge of protection around you (Job 1:10). Two things: the devil has to ask permission to sift you or will try to lure you by the use of temptations and perverted desires to get you to step out of God's protection.

<u>Sift:</u>

- to isolate or separate that which is most important or useful.
- to remove lumps or large particles in a sieve

While the devil meant it for harm, God uses the sifting for His good. Do not be distracted by the tactics of the enemy. Focus on Jesus. The reason God allows for separation is that you are not like those who oppose you, God does not want you to be influenced by the world but focused on Him. Isolation is just for a season. It is meant for you to go deeper with God. God never leaves us or forsakes us (Deuteronomy 31:6). The devil wants to sift you to kill you. God uses the sifting to remove the nasty things on our hearts like bitterness, anger, and selfish things to show you what truly matters. God removes what can be shaken--that is, created things--so that what cannot be shaken may remain (Hebrews 12:27). The demonic attacks were meant for evil, but God used them for His good. Do not despise a season of isolation. It is teaching you to lean on Jesus. During this time of isolation, you will get the most spiritual growth and development. God will teach you and show you things that He would not be able to gift you with if you were distracted. From the Old Testament (Joshua, David, etc.) to the New Testament (Jesus, John, etc.) God would hide people for a certain time right before they were revealed to the public.

Each of them carried a revelation that God had given them that was to impact regions and nations in isolated places. Your isolation is protection and preparation for a shift and breakthrough in your life. It is to prepare you for the assignment God has for your life.

Daniel 10:12 (NIV)

Then he continued, "Do not be afraid, Daniel. Since the first day that you set your mind to gain understanding and to humble yourself before your God (fasted, prayed), your words were heard, and I have come in response to them.

When things are changing, and it feels uncomfortable because we know a shift is happening. Start fasting. Fasting will help you to rid yourself of last season's junk. Fasting is a discipline in both the Old and New Testament that helps you humble yourself before God. Fasting also helps you position and prepare your heart for what God is about to do. When you pray and fast together, it is really powerful. Some supernatural breakthroughs, doors of opportunity, or connections cannot happen unless you pray and fast (Mark 9:14-29). Daniel fasted food, he only ate from food that came from a seed (fruits, vegetables, grains, water). When Daniel fasted, God gave him supernatural insight, vision, protection, and everything Daniel needed to survive in a land of captivity. If food is hard for health reasons, fast your words and prepare yourself to be silent before the Lord ready to listen. Fast from bitter grudges in your heart and start the process to reconcile. Search all that is within you to forgive and ask God to forgive you, too. Fast the thoughts in your mind that see a reason to complain, start opening your eyes to blessings all around you that you are thankful for. Fast your doubt and place yourself in a position to hope and believe God will change every situation around. In a time of transition, you have to let things die for new things to grow in your life. Jesus commanded us to pick up our crosses and walk with Him (Luke 9:23). This is what He is asking you to do. Die to your sin. Die to your fleshly temptations, be born again with a new mind and a new heart. It is a new season, so humble yourself before the Lord. Maybe fast from social media to separate yourself from the distractions of your online community, put your focus toward this new season to start planning out your vision. All the toxic stuff of the old season has to go. King David in the Old Testament asked God to make him right with God requesting, "Create in me a clean heart, O God, and renew a right and steadfast spirit within me" (Psalm 51:10). That might have to be your prayer for a while, for God to break the chains of wrong motives.

Romans 5:3b-5a (NIV)

"… we know that suffering produces perseverance; perseverance, character; and character, hope. And hope does not put us to shame …"

You can approach God. God loves you. The devil is always a liar. He will make you think that you are unworthy to come to God. The truth is Jesus gave you access to the throne room of God. When Jesus died on the cross, his blood was shed over your sins. God does not see your sins that the devil will accuse you of. God sees Jesus. There is power in the blood of Jesus. The blood of Jesus washed you clean of the enemy's filth. Through Jesus, you have access to be in God's presence. In God's presence, there is fullness of joy (Psalm 16:11). In God's presence, all the pressures and trials do not matter. As long as we stay with the right spirit, right motives, and right heart, God takes care of the rest. Keep your words in praise of God. As long as you are magnifying God, not the problem, the problem will seize. You come this far by faith, leaning on the Lord, trusting in His Holy Word, God never fails. Your words are powerful. As soon as you open your mouth you have life and death in the power of your tongue. The moment you speak God's name in praise, thanksgiving, and worship, the enemy loses its power over you.

2 Corinthians 4:8-9 (NIV)

"We are hard-pressed on every side, but not crushed; perplexed, but not in despair; persecuted, but not abandoned; struck down, but not destroyed."

God has given you the courage to fight the good fight of faith (1 Timothy 6:12). The main way to break any chain is by watching the words you say about yourself, about your children, about your life. Stop saying you are broke. Stop telling yourself that you are not good enough. Stop complaining and speaking words that make you a victim. Stop talking about the drama. All you are doing is fueling the fire and blocking your blessing. If you are going to fight for your life to change, you have to change your words. Your words change your heart. Your heart changes your mind. God said renew your mind (Romans 12:2). The words of your mouth have power. The ultimate test of faith is if you can praise God when you are going through the worst times.

The name that is above every name is Jesus, who is all-powerful. Jesus said, "I am the way the truth and the life. No one reaches the father unless they go through me" (John 14:6). That means Jesus is the way out of bondage. Jesus is the way to your blessing. Speak the name of Jesus over every area of your life. Take back the region, your bloodline, the neighborhood, and the nation and speak Jesus's name over all of it and break the chains. You are no longer bound; you are free in Jesus's name. Jesus knows the way to get your life in order. Speak life to your future. Speak the truth to yourself and your family. You are the head and not the tail (Deuteronomy 28:13). Yes, Jesus is the way out of poverty and into financial security. Yes, Jesus is the way out of lack into more than enough. Jesus is your source. You are going to have to speak the words of truth that Jesus spoke over every circumstance. The moment you start praising the name of Jesus, every chain will break. The power of God is loosed, your enemies have shut their mouths and watch you get blessed and God gets the glory. Don't talk about your enemies, don't even bring up the situation, do not even react although it's hard. Focus on Jesus as if none of it is happening and start praising. Every day, trust God and praise Him. Every day exalt Him through the pain. Every day give thanks to Him while you cry. Every day praise Him through the sickness. Everyday worship Him through the heaviness of your heart. Even if your daily prayer is just His name, then pray "Jesus!" with all your might. There is power in the name of Jesus. Every demon must flee when you speak His name. Jesus is the way to freedom, follow Him.

Psalm 118:5-6 (ESV)

"Out of my distress I called on the LORD; the LORD answered me and set me free. The LORD is on my side; I will not fear. What can man do to me?"

CHAPTER 10
GOD'S MIRACLES

1 Peter 2:9 (NIV)

But you are a chosen people, a royal priesthood, a holy nation, God's special possession, that you may declare the praises of him who called you out of darkness into his wonderful light.

You have an opportunity to start fresh. Remember, there's nothing in your past to go back for. You have a new life in Jesus, and your past must be buried along with your sin. God called you a chosen person, royal, and a part of His holy nation. God's promises are precious and magnificent, for you to experience His divine nature (2 Peter 1:4). When you are chosen by God, you inherit His promises. God's promises are there for you to claim over all that is connected to you. God's promises are there to increase our belief that God is true and increase our faith. Each believer will understand the value of God's promises through patience and persistent prayer. We learn to give honor to God who proves every word is true.

We seek to know truth and truth that sets people free. "For this is good and acceptable in the sight of God our Savior, who desires all men to be saved and to come to the knowledge of the truth" 1 Timothy 2:3-4. The word in Hebrew for "truth" is *amet*. It means to be totally honest and transparent. Jesus is transparent in the thoughts He has for us which are good and not evil (Jeremiah 29:11). God's transparency is in the hidden deep places searching one's heart and knowing when they sit down and stand up (Psalm 139:1-2). The Lord is transparent in knowing our thoughts and the hairs on our heads (Luke 12:7). The bible is transparent when it says nothing is hidden from God (Hebrews 4:13). The truth is God is with you wherever you go (Joshua 1:9). It is true God gives us beauty in exchange for our ashes, joy instead of mourning, praise instead of despair

(Isaiah 61:3). That means God knows what you need. The pattern of the Lord before a miracle was to cleanse a person's soul of sin, testing their faith, then the miracle mending process began.

Joshua 21:45 (NIV)

Not one of all the Lord's good promises to Israel failed; everyone was fulfilled.

The blood of Jesus promised to blot out every sin you have ever made and remember them no more (Isaiah 43:25). Jesus died on the cross and rose from the dead for you to have eternal freedom for your soul. The saving grace of the Lord has given us hope in Jesus for this lifetime and eternity. Eternity seems so far away. Tomorrow is not promised. In a split second, you are here today and gone tomorrow. The blood of Jesus is everlasting; the promises of God are eternal. They never end and are always true. When Jesus shed His blood, He forgave you, He crossed out your sin to be no more.

Psalm 103:3 (NIV)

who forgives all your sins and heals all your diseases,

God promises to heal our mind, our body, and our spirit. Thirty-seven miracles were recorded in the Bible that Jesus fulfilled. Throughout the whole Bible, people were healed of, not just physical ailments, but of emotional bondage, mental health, delivered from demons and even raised people from the dead. Jesus spoke to each sickness, disease, and spirit behind the oppression and commanded it to "GO!" Jesus said, "Go, be healed." Complete healing was accomplished because each person had faith in the work of Jesus for either their personal healing or on behalf of someone else that believed God is a healer (Exodus 15:26). The key was their faith, and it was established. Even today, there are miracles of complete healing that opposed expert medical diagnosis because people believed Jesus is a Great Physician who healed their body, mind, and spirit better than it was before any sickness entered their body. Even today miracles still happen where tumors have fallen off of people's bodies, demons are being cast out of people, and the oppressed in their minds are being set free. There are times when angels have appeared to people in their times of need of protection. Numbers and time in themselves are infinite. Even in nature, God does wonders on the earth that either scares or mesmerizes scientists of the unexplainable things of the creation of the world. Like a flower that grows, dies for a season, and then comes back to life in another moment, whose seeds fall to the ground and produce a field harvest of flowerbeds for the world to enjoy.

Mark 9:23

Jesus said to him, "If you can believe,
all things are possible to him who believes."

Your faith activates God's miracles. Do not doubt in your heart and mind. Hebrews 10:23 says do not waiver because God is faithful. God is faithful to fulfill every promise made to you. Your faith activates your divine healing. Your faith activates your divine deliverance. I say "divine" because when it happens, it will be in a way that man cannot accomplish or take credit for turning your situation around. You believed God would give you a child and He opened your womb when you were not able to have kids. You believed you were not going to be paralyzed from the accident and now you can walk despite the medical report because your faith in God believed in His healing power. You were pronounced dead and on life-support, but God did not allow them to pull the cord because you were going to make it through. God stopped you from walking into that party where gunshots were fired because God protected you. You went two weeks without any money and

God sat you in the right room to nail that job interview that pays all your bills because God is a Provider. You almost lost your mind fighting that war, but PTSD symptoms vanished because God gave you peace and took that anxiety out of you. Your miracle is in God, your faith to believe that God can and will do it. Remember who God is. He is a Healer, He is a Deliverer, He is a Provider. He is all things that divinely turn your life around.

Isaiah 14:24 (NIV)

The Lord Almighty has sworn,
"Surely, as I have planned, so it will be,
and as I have purposed, so it will happen."

God's miracles and promises are a sure thing. It is a done deal. Surely goodness and mercy follow me all the days of my life (Psalm 23:6). Surely God is my help; the Lord is the one who sustains me (Psalm 54:4). He helps you. Surely, he will rescue you from every trap and protect you from deadly disease (Psalms 91:3). He keeps you healthy. God's Word also says, "I will surely bless you and give you many descendants" (Hebrews 6:14). He multiplies you. God surely does what He says. What God says is part of the plan He has for your life (Isaiah 14:24).

Jeremiah 29:11-13

For I know the plans I have for you," declares the Lord, "plans to prosper you and not to harm you, plans to give you hope and a future. Then you will call on me and come and pray to me, and I will listen to you. You will seek me and find me when you seek me with all your heart."

Your deliverance is a miracle. God took your life to use as a testimony for someone else. Your life is a miracle. What you went through is a miracle. Do not be afraid to open your mouth and share your story. You are an inspiration. You are a survivor.

You are an overcomer. There is going to be a moment when we come face to face with our old selves. At that moment, we will realize as we tell our story how God brought us through. Not just that we made it through, but how God blessed us along the way. How God was there through it all. How God transformed us for our good.

God does supernatural things in our day-to-day life. You woke up this morning. There is someone around this world that did not wake up this morning. The flowers grow and bloom, die, and then grow and bloom again. These are the miracles we take for granted. As we go through battles, trials, temptations, and all kinds of things that life gives. God is our refuge and strength in all kinds of times of trouble (Psalm 46:1). God surrounds us with favor (Psalm 5:12) and is our shield of protection (Psalm 18:2). God is our peace that calms our storms (Psalm 107:29).

Psalms 140:13

Surely the righteous shall give thanks unto thy name:
the upright shall dwell in thy presence.

Remember to acknowledge God in all things. Remember God when He blesses you. Remember when He healed you. Remember when He helped you. Remember God when He pulled you out of a mess. This chapter is for you to rest, reflect, and remember all the things God has done. When you wake in the morning and when you go to bed at night, these are times of reflection. Thank God as you remember the times you laughed and the times you cried. God was working in your tears, too.

Psalm 107:30-31

They were glad when it grew calm,
and he guided them to their desired haven.
Let them give thanks to the Lord for his unfailing love

and his wonderful deeds for mankind.

It is important to rest in God. There are going to be tough days. We are going to have to build ourselves up and encourage ourselves to build our faith. We cannot depend on other people's affirmations to cheer us on. You have to tell yourself who God is to you. Remember His promises, remember who He is in you and how you are portraying His image. It is also a time to reassess where you are, where you have been, and where you are going. As you reflect on forgiveness, health, finances, your home, relationship, necessities, and your emotions, remember God is with you always even as you are processing all the areas of your life. Ask yourself where God has been in these areas. If you don't see it, ask God to enter into areas where you feel there is a lack. Ask God to step into an area that needs to be made whole or renewed. Rest in God. Rest in His stillness and in the silence. Posture your heart in gratitude to thank God. As you sit and rest, I give you this psalm and promises to help you rest, reflect, and remember the goodness of God.

Psalm 19:8-14 (NIV)

The precepts of the Lord are right,
giving joy to the heart.
The commands of the Lord are radiant,
giving light to the eyes.
The fear of the Lord is pure,
enduring forever.
The decrees of the Lord are firm,
and all of them are righteous.

They are more precious than gold,
than much pure gold;
they are sweeter than honey,

than honey from the honeycomb.
By them your servant is warned;
in keeping them there is great reward.
But who can discern their own errors?
Forgive my hidden faults.
Keep your servant also from willful sins;
may they not rule over me.
Then I will be blameless,
innocent of great transgression.
May these words of my mouth and this meditation of my heart
be pleasing in your sight,
Lord, *my Rock and my Redeemer.*

CHAPTER 11
YOUR IDENTITY IN CHRIST

Ephesians 2:10 (AMP)

"For we are God's [own] handiwork (His workmanship), recreated in Christ Jesus, [born anew] that we may do those good works which God predestined (planned beforehand) for us [taking paths which He prepared ahead of time], that we should walk in them [living the good life which He prearranged and made ready for us to live]..."

Sometimes when people go through or are born into trauma, the impact paralyzes them in a place they are not supposed to be. They get comfortable in dysfunctional environments, mindsets, and behaviors that trap them in a fear that stops them from going after something better. It is hard for one to break free from the lies they were told that said they were less than who they are. Social media presents people who have it all together. We never see the struggle or truth behind the pictures. The truth is you are God's workmanship. You are the product of the beauty of God's craftsmanship. He personally molded us as a potter to clay (Isaiah 64:8). By the grace of God, we have been fashioned according to His image, given access to do predestined works that are divine mysteries to the natural mind. God gave us a Christ-like mind (1 Corinthians 2:16). A life that we are instructed to walk in, that we can enjoy, change atmospheres and take dominion. In our mother's womb, we became His unique masterpiece, special and precious to Him. Daily we are in the process to become better versions of ourselves according to God's will. Despite insecurities, we were created with greatness on the inside. We are not to be held back but to come forth out of the shadows and into the light (Job 12:22).

Isaiah 43:1 (NIV)

"But now, this is what the LORD says — he who created you, Jacob, he who formed you, Israel: 'Do not fear, for I have redeemed you; I have summoned you by name; you are mine.'"

When out on the streets we meet so many people. The most loving people you will ever meet are in places you least expect, one is homeless tent cities. Sure, they landed on tough times. One thing is that their value is one another. When they lost everything, an understanding of what is truly valuable became more important. That is love. Even though they live a life that seems forgotten. The moment we share God's love and that they matter, you see the beauty of hope breaks through. The tears in their eyes that yes, God loves you. No, you are not forgotten. God's love perfectly accepts you right where you are. Sometimes we feel forgotten or exempt from the love of God. That is not true. God loves you right where you are. He has plans for your life beyond what you can ever ask, imagine, or think (Ephesians 3:20).

God loves you. He loves you so much He sent His Son on the cross to die so He could have a relationship with you. Jesus died to seal that relationship, but He also rose from the dead and is alive to continue His good work in you. God wants to show you how truly special you are. God desires to honor, respect, and value (1 Peter 2:17) you so much that He blesses and trusts you with gifts and talents that are heavenly (Matthew 7:11). God loves you so much He wants your face to be radiant with His glory that makes you attractive to those who don't know Him (2 Corinthians 3:18). God loves you so much He wants you to step into rooms and change the atmosphere (2 Chronicles 5:13-14). God will never take his love from you; in fact, God wants to pour out His love upon you like rain (Romans 5:5). He loves you so much He is patient, gentle, and kind, even in His corrections (Colossians 3:12-14). God loves you, He made you to be a vessel in this world for His Kingdom (2 Timothy 2:21). You have value and purpose because He loves you. You are his child; you are precious and valuable (Galatians 4:7). You matter. You were made for such a time as this (Esther 4:14). Allow God to move the pieces of your life around so you can shine.

Jeremiah 6:27 (NIV)

"I have made you a tester of metals
and my people the ore,
that you may observe
and test their ways.
You have greatness inside of you."

God made you to be a witness everywhere to shake things up and bring the power of God like never before. He sent you to take your stance of dominion wherever you are because you carry His glory. The devil is scared of being pushed out of his comfort of controlling territories he stole. That is why he sends people to discredit the work you are building. We are instructed to take dominion and step into our position to be revolutionary in this world that follows routine patterns. God set you apart to be a leader. We do not have to give in to the world system of validation through social media. You have nothing to prove except being obedient to God. You set your position to God's truth of who you are, and God does the rest to promote you. Your purpose is weighty. The best part is when God takes you from the back of the line into the front. He takes every broken piece and restores it. God fights for you; what He started in you to build He will finish. God has your back no matter what it looks like (Deuteronomy 30:3-13). God does not give you easy things. He gives you people, assignments, and projects that require you to act in faith, not the easiness of simplicity. For God to work the best miracles, blessings, and breakthroughs in our lives, we have to step out of our comfort zone and trust God in the unknown, lose control, and let God work out all the details.

Genesis 1:26-28 King James Version (KJV)

And God said, Let us make man in our image, after our likeness: and let them have dominion over the fish of the sea, and over the fowl of the air, and over the cattle, and over all the earth, and over every creeping thing that creepeth upon the earth.

So God created man in his own image, in the image of God created he him; male and female created he them.

And God blessed them, and God said unto them, Be fruitful, and multiply, and replenish the earth, and subdue it: and have dominion over the fish of the sea, and over the fowl of the air, and over every living thing that moveth upon the earth.

Bishop Tudor Bismark from Zimbabwe laid this out in his teaching *The Order of the Kingdom.*

Seven basic kingdoms that affect us:

1. Sovereign - Where God rules, God's throne room, courtroom

2. Angelic/Celestial - Seraphim, cherubim, thrones, dominations or dominions, virtues, powers, principalities or princedoms, archangels, angels & demons

3. Planetary - Sun, moon, stars, galactic systems, comets, solar system

4. Man - Humans, Male, Female

5. Animal - Birds of the air, fish in the sea, beasts on the ground

6. Plants - Trees, weeds, moss, seaweed, fruits, vegetables, nuts, grains, flowers

7. Mineral - Copper, gold, silver, bronze, rubies, diamonds, salt, clay, coal, oil/gas, sulfur, water

We were created to take dominion on earth (Genesis 1:26). We are not supposed to worship the stars, "energy" gemstones, animal bones, thousand-year-old trees, or wise human beings who ultimately die. We were created to worship God alone (Luke 4:8). We were instructed to seek the Kingdom of God first (Matthew 6:33) Sovereign throne room where God and Jesus are seated. Then all these other things, all these other kingdoms, will be given to you. We have to seek the strategies, processes, thoughts, and ideas of the Kingdom of God to take dominion in other areas of our life.

For instance, where does money come from? Cash comes from 75% cotton and 25% linen (fibers of the flax plant) and coins come from copper, zinc, and nickel. If you are only seeking money, you are operating in the lowest kingdom level and never have influence or structure in the other kingdom realms. You will never know how to take dominion over demonic attacks or learn how to change atmospheres because you are only understanding how to operate in a lesser area. If you want influence in the supernatural and the natural to heal the sick and raise the dead, cast out demons (Matthew 10:8), visions (Acts 2:17), and call things that are not (Romans 4:16-22), seek the Kingdom of God first, THEN, all the other things will be given to you. Our first ask in prayer would be to know the mind of Christ and the heart of Christ. All these other mysteries of the Kingdom. All these other doors of influence in every level. Access to all these areas to change and shift things for the Kingdom of God. Your greatness comes from God. Once God pours out His Spirit upon us to operate in these areas, then money will chase after you. But to whom much is given, much will be required (Luke 12:48). What Jesus did then still happen today through those who fervently seek the Kingdom of God.

Romans 11:29 (AMP)

For the gifts and the calling of God are irrevocable [for He does not withdraw what He has given, nor does He change His mind about those to whom He gives His grace or to whom He sends His call].

When God created us, He appointed us to be knowledgeable, talented, gifted in certain areas of expertise. This is where you lay your head (Matthew 8:20), your thoughts, and your ideas. Some people know from childhood exactly what they were meant to do, and others have to discover their purpose in later stages of their life. Even though we can do all things through Christ (Philippians 4:13), He did not say we can do everything, although some people are well versed in many things. I cannot play the saxophone. I could if I was taught but that is not my place of dominion. We have to know our place otherwise we will be out of order. Your calling is in the things that bring you joy, in your God-given talents, the things that spark your motivation to pursue. When you are called by God, your calling does not necessarily mean to pastor a church. Your calling could be with your own family, or group of friends, even on your job. The skills that God gave you will give you access to people whom God called you to minister or help. God will put you with the right people, right time, in the right place for you to share or be an example of God's love. Once God sets your calling into motion, it is irrevocable. It will not stop until you complete the task. You cannot run from it and you cannot quit. God will chase you down like He did Jonah. God assigned the winds, the waves, and a whale to bring Jonah back to God's mission to save the city of Nineveh. God does not change His mind. God called you to an assignment that has value and brings God glory. Even if it means trusting to love the unlovable. To befriend the most difficult or unpopular. Or to give when it is hard to give. Or adopt the parentless. There is just as much of a reward in the private callings as there are in the public assignment. Everything does not need to be posted on social media for God to use you in a mighty way. God's call is not meant to entertain the world; it is meant to save the world from eternal damnation. God sees the things you have done for His glory, that is what matters. God's call is not open for judgment; the call is open for fulfillment.

Our identity is not our job, how much money we have, social media likes, or a title to our name. Outward vanities are not whom God says you are. Your identity is in Christ. Your significance is in Jesus. When people are asked who they are, they either proudly brag or answer humbly. Whatever you identify yourself as your intimacy with Jesus will reveal levels of yourself as a new creation in every season. You are constantly a work in progress. There is no end to who God is, and as He is so are you (1 John 4:17). When people ask who you are, that answer should be a child of God, I believe in Christ.

I always have a pen and a paper with me because no matter where I am, there is always an opportunity to learn. When someone is speaking, there is always an opportunity to take in at least one thing that someone has just poured into you. You have to be willing to be open. Take the things people applied to you and make them your own, even if it is not words but behaviors. Do not copy them but personalize them to fit your structure and character. Be content in correction. Constructive criticism is great. Even if we couldn't use the advice at that moment, we can still take their advice for another season where we can use it. This is all part of the development.

The disciples were discovering their identity when they followed Jesus. They either had to watch, learn, listen or perform everything that Jesus was doing, followed by a series of questions that made them think deeper as to what Jesus instructed them to do. Jesus would give constructive criticism to the disciples on many occasions for their development in preparation for the disciples to go on their own to all ends of the earth. The disciples took a three-year crash course on Jesus and the Kingdom of God. Their teachings set the stage for the foundation of the church. The signs and wonders they performed were the evidence to let unbelievers know that the Kingdom of God was here. The Gospels teach us the life of Jesus, as the disciples were learners, so we are to be learners as well.

Now the Holy Spirit that lives inside of us gives us energy that enables us to do miraculous things for the Kingdom of God. The Holy Spirit enables us to have wisdom and skills for supernatural tasks. The works of our hands are prosperous by the power of the Holy Spirit. We have a mighty powerful energy source of God within us that is ready to be activated by the words spoken from our mouths. When we speak "I am healed," we are speaking healing coming onto us. When we speak "I am prosperous," we are speaking prosperity to come to us. When we pray and speak things into existence, what we speak is what we attract. When we are calling things to us, we are also calling in opposition. When we pray and ask God, "God give me wisdom," the Holy Spirit jumps into action and gives us divine wisdom. The enemy also comes in to try to make us feel insecure in our knowledge. The enemy does not want us to have vision because he wants us to die (Proverbs 29:18). When we say, "I am broke," the Holy Spirit cannot do anything because we are speaking death to come to our finances. But Jesus said, "I am the way, the truth, and the life" (John 14:6). "Holy Spirit is a helper" (John 14:26). You have power in you to manifest greatness into your life. We have to build it, go from glory to Glory and faith to Faith. We do not just take one word of instruction from the Bible and run with it. No, we must keep going deeper, keep growing, keep learning. It does not matter your age.

What we call into existence will happen if it is according to God's will. We cannot call forth riches just to be selfishly rich. God created us to be a blessing. We are not to be careless in our blessing. This is why we all need supervision; we need to be under a pastor. The pastor has authority from God to pour out wisdom and direction to us. A pastor should be highly honored and respected because he has been given the authority by God to watch over us and the body of believers as our guardian shepherd. Our pastor is our spiritual covering. The pastor receives wisdom, mysteries, strategies, and instructions to pour into us. We are sheep that assemble; the pastor is a shepherd. Everyone should be in a church to learn and receive wisdom, knowledge, and understanding. Everyone should be under a pastor who guides and teaches them to go out into the world to be witnesses. The covering we are under should be sufficient for our call.

If we become rich, we should give back. God does not want us to be poor. God supplies all of our needs. All of what God gives us is to be a blessing for someone else to be a testimony of faith. To do the works of the Kingdom, not selfish gain. What God gives He can also take away. If He takes something away, it is for our edification not for punishment. God wants us to operate in His power with the right motives. God called us to be a witness of His Kingdom in our home, on the job, and at school or wherever we set our foot to share the Gospel of Christ. God is making us living evidence of His glory to share what He has done for us He can do for others. We are a witness to testify to the glory of God to change the atmosphere and be a person of influence for the Kingdom of God.

Proverbs 31:10-31 (NIV)

Epilogue: The Wife of Noble Character

A wife of noble character who can find?
She is worth far more than rubies.
Her husband has full confidence in her
and lacks nothing of value.
She brings him good, not harm,
all the days of her life.
She selects wool and flax
and works with eager hands.
She is like the merchant ships,
bringing her food from afar.
She gets up while it is still night;
she provides food for her family
and portions for her female servants.
She considers a field and buys it;
out of her earnings she plants a vineyard.
She sets about her work vigorously;
her arms are strong for her tasks.
She sees that her trading is profitable,
and her lamp does not go out at night.
In her hand she holds the distaff
and grasps the spindle with her fingers.
She opens her arms to the poor
and extends her hands to the needy.
When it snows, she has no fear for her household;
for all of them are clothed in scarlet.
She makes coverings for her bed;
she is clothed in fine linen and purple.
Her husband is respected at the city gate,
where he takes his seat among the elders of the land.
She makes linen garments and sells them,

and supplies the merchants with sashes.
She is clothed with strength and dignity;
she can laugh at the days to come.
She speaks with wisdom,
and faithful instruction is on her tongue.
She watches over the affairs of her household
and does not eat the bread of idleness.
Her children arise and call her blessed;
her husband also, and he praises her:
"Many women do noble things,
but you surpass them all."
Charm is deceptive, and beauty is fleeting;
but a woman who fears the Lord is to be praised.
Honor her for all that her hands have done,
and let her works bring her praise at the city gate.

Solomon paints this picture of the perfect woman. In actuality, it is not a singular woman. Solomon was painting a picture of the church. The church of Christ is often represented as a woman in the Bible; the church is the "bride of Christ" (2 Corinthians 11:2), and Israel is the "wife of Yahweh/God" (Isaiah 54:5) (Revelation 19:7). All of these characteristics are whom we are supposed to be: strength, dignity, and prosperity in all of these ways. What God is saying is we are people of honor and nobility everywhere we go.

Matthew 5:13-16 (NIV)

Salt and Light

"You are the salt of the earth. But if the salt loses its saltiness, how can it be made salty again? It is no longer good for anything, except to be thrown out and trampled underfoot.

"You are the light of the world. A town built on a hill cannot be hidden. Neither do people light a lamp and put it under a bowl. Instead, they put it on its stand, and it gives light to everyone in the house. In the same way, let your light shine before others, that they may see your good deeds and glorify your Father in heaven.

You are salt and light in the world. Salt is a preservative and also adds flavor. Light illuminates what is hidden in the dark. God preserves us; God is saying He protects and covers us. He makes us flavorful and attractive to illuminate the goodness of God in dark places. We bring in light where there was darkness. We remove the veil of things that are hidden. However, Jesus also mentioned, if His followers were to lose their saltiness, they would no longer be effective at protecting and amplifying God's goodness in the world. Our effectiveness starts in our home. Be salt and light in your home. Preserving the God-given goodness that brings unity and love in the home and exposing the hidden dark places that God says to toss out. Get every evil thing out of your house. Do not allow any evil influences to come into your home.

Joshua 24:15 (NIV)

But if serving the Lord seems undesirable to you, then choose for yourselves this day whom you will serve, whether the gods your ancestors served beyond the Euphrates, or the gods of the Amorites, in whose land you are living. But as for me and my household, we will serve the Lord."

God doesn't bless watchers, God blesses doers (Proverbs 6:6). Do not bring pride into your calling. The presence of God will not compete with your arrogance. Our purpose has a purpose. Diligently walking in our purpose by faith so that we are fruitful to multiply. Like Psalm 143:10 says, "Teach me to do your will…" God honors those who serve Him (John 12:26). Service is a part of worship and you are a worshiper unto God. Know that the movement of God is always progressive. We have to be ready to move when God moves. God moved by a cloud by day and fire at night (Exodus 13:21). You got to keep moving and following God each day. Remember, you are now a child of the living God.

Galatians 3:26

You are all sons of God through faith in Christ Jesus.

CHAPTER 12
VICTORY & DEFEAT

Matthew 5:1-12 (NIV)

Sermon on the Mount

Now when Jesus saw the crowds, he went up on a mountainside and sat down. His disciples came to him, and he began to teach them.

The Beatitudes

He said:
"Blessed are the poor in spirit,
for theirs is the kingdom of heaven.
Blessed are those who mourn,
for they will be comforted.
Blessed are the meek,
for they will inherit the earth.
Blessed are those who hunger and thirst for righteousness,
for they will be filled.
Blessed are the merciful,
for they will be shown mercy.
Blessed are the pure in heart,
for they will see God.
Blessed are the peacemakers,
for they will be called children of God.
Blessed are those who are persecuted because of righteousness,
for theirs is the kingdom of heaven.

"Blessed are you when people insult you, persecute you and falsely say all kinds of evil against you because of me. Rejoice and be glad, because great is your reward in heaven, for in the same way they persecuted the prophets who were before you."

Victory and defeat really is a battle of our mind. Our perspective will determine either one or the other. With God, He looks at the motives of our minds and the posture of our hearts. We are transformed by the renewing of our minds (Romans 12:2). Until we change our thinking, we will always recycle our experiences. When Jesus talked about being blessed, he addressed blessings in the most unique way. The "beatitudes" means happy and blissful. Blessed means many different things, in this case, if we follow Jesus, here are the Kingdom keys to happiness. I would say provision and protection because that is what generally multiplies for the fruitfulness of order. God is a God of order. God will not step into chaos. Blessings are the overflow of being whole and optimistic. Optimism is not being happy. Optimism is seeing a great outcome past the obstacles to victory. In these blessings, Jesus was saying that we are favored, healthy, privileged, esteemed, honored, admirable, and overcomers. All nine of the blessings confront, by the grace of God, successfully achieving the conditions of a person's heart who walks in the obedience of God. These are those who will receive a blessing ultimately reach levels of happiness within their blessings, being content in all situations.

1. **Blessed are the poor in spirit, for theirs is the kingdom of heaven.**

    a. Blessed in this case is "to be envied." People are going to be jealous because of your walk with God.

    b. Poor in spirit means lacking spiritually, it is also a posture of humility (laying your pride down) because your dependence is on God who is your provider. Adam Clarke's commentary says, "spiritual poverty and wretchedness." It is a posture that addresses one's salvation. Kind of like the song Amazing Grace, "Who saved a wretch like me."

   c. Reward: Kingdom of heaven - eternal reward when you receive Christ. There is only one way to heaven and that is through Christ.

2. **Blessed are they who mourn, for they will be comforted.**

   a. Morn: deep conviction or feeling guilty. You are sensitive to sinful nature.

   b. Will be comforted: actually, means to draw near. God will call you unto himself.

   c. This is addressing the promise that God forgives you of your sins. This is your testimony of encouragement that you are redeemed.

3. **Blessed are the meek, for they will inherit the land / earth.**

   a. Meek: be humble - putting your pride aside. It's also saying self-controlled.

   b. Will inherit: possess, comes from God, He is giving you something from Him.

   c. Reward: Being in maximum content of true joy in all conditions of life through the abundance of God's provision as a vindication that God alone supplies all your needs.

4. **Blessed are they who hunger and thirst for righteousness, for they will be satisfied / fulfilled.**

   a. Hunger and thirst: mean to desire earnestly to possess the whole thing; not part of it, pursue God first as a priority, actively seeking God.

b. Righteousness: means justification, right standing, will not compromise their character, purity.

c. Fulfilled, completely satisfied. Sense of moral and spiritual satisfaction. Stability of the promise, that this satisfaction is a sure thing.

5. **Blessed are the merciful, for they will be shown mercy.**

a. Merciful: compassionate, disposition of the heart, through which it is affected. WHILE in pain, miseries, grievous.

b. Reward: compassion; divine grace, forgiveness.

c. Choosing forgiveness over hate.

6. **Blessed are the clean/pure of heart, for they will see God.**

a. Pure of heart: unstained with the guilt of anything, free from corrupt desire and shame from sin.

b. Heart: in spirit, good conscience and motives.

c. See: possess God, possession of eternal glory, walk by faith, the security of belief in what is unseen in the natural. Blessed because to see God satisfies the longings of the heart with special favor.

7. **Blessed are the peacemakers, for they will be called children of God.**

a. Peacemaker: reconciliation/restoration/ unity with 1) God, 2) self 3) people | to defuse disunity/ discord / war.

b. Be called: recognized as.

   c. Children of God: resemble God's character, image, and likeness.

8. **Blessed are they who are persecuted for the sake of righteousness, for theirs is the kingdom of heaven.**

   a. Persecuted: cruel and unjust hostile pursuit / make run away through mistreatment / drive away through harassment.

   b. Sake of righteousness: Not for any crimes they have done | separate themselves from the world | loyalty to the Kingdom of heaven.

   c. Kingdom of heaven: eternal reward.

9. **Blessed are you when people insult you, persecute you and falsely say all kinds of evil against you because of me.**

   a. Same as above persecution plus outward violence, rejection, slander, lies, and manipulation.

   b. All kinds of evil: the worst things they could think of and invent.

   c. Because of me: loyalty to Jesus.

10. **Rejoice and be glad, because great is your reward in heaven, for in the same way they persecuted the prophets who were before you.**

   a. Be glad: extremely glad promised you will see.

   b. Great is your reward in heaven: To those who suffer most (such as martyrdom), God imparts the highest rewards.

c. Prophets who were before you: dignity was true to the responsibility to speak the Word of God, in this case, speak the Gospel.

The Bible talks about being blessed in many different ways. Blessings are not always material things, but bigger rewards for our souls that are eternal after we have passed from this earth. Come to find out even though we are blessed, there are many hardships. It is almost inevitable that as soon as God blesses us; there is opposition one way or another. When we face opposition, we have either 1) defeated something that was meant to keep us bound, passing the test, or 2) we are extremely close to our breakthrough, and the enemy wants to stop us from achieving our reward. Our opposition is a sign of something good. If we were not facing opposition, we might want to wonder if we are going on the right path because it is too comfortable. "Blessed are you when people insult you, persecute you and falsely say all kinds of evil against you because of me." This says blessing is going to get ugly the closer you are to Jesus, but the uglier the situation we receive the grandest and ultimate rewards and blessings. The bigger the trial, the bigger the blessing.

As soon as the angel told Mary she was blessed and highly favored; surprise! you're pregnant, the next minute she was running for her life because people wanted to kill the baby inside of her, who was Jesus (Luke 1). Mary had to run away a few times to protect her blessing, Jesus. Blessings come with a price. People want our blessings but do not want to pay the price we went through to get the blessing. Remember it is not about us, it is about Jesus and the Kingdom of heaven, the work that He is doing in us and through us is transformational. Jesus said they hated Him first (John 15:18-27). Jesus had to remind the disciples of the attacks they suffered. It was not them they were after; it was the greatness of the Kingdom assignment they were attached to that the world and flesh despised.

Ephesians 6:10-18 (NIV)
The Armor of God

Finally, be strong in the Lord and in his mighty power. Put on the full armor of God, so that you can take your stand against the devil's schemes. For our struggle is not against flesh and blood, but against the rulers, against the authorities, against the powers of this dark world and against the spiritual forces of evil in the heavenly realms. Therefore, put on the full armor of God, so that when the day of evil comes, you may be able to stand your ground, and after you have done everything, to stand. Stand firm then, with the belt of truth buckled around your waist, with the breastplate of righteousness in place, and with your feet fitted with the readiness that comes from the gospel of peace. In addition to all this, take up the shield of faith, with which you can extinguish all the flaming arrows of the evil one. Take the helmet of salvation and the sword of the Spirit, which is the word of God. And pray in the Spirit on all occasions with all kinds of prayers and requests. With this in mind, be alert and always keep on praying for all the Lord's people.

Put on the full armor of God. You are in a spiritual battle zone. There is spiritual warfare all around. God is in heaven and God needs a vessel on earth to perform His will for the Kingdom to come on earth as it is in heaven. The devil does the same thing. The devil needs a vessel to use to operate kingdom darkness on earth as it is in hell which is eternal torment (Matthew 13:42). You have this battle between good and evil. Since the gates of hell are not opened until the final judgment and the last days (Revelation 20), the earth is evil's battlefield.

Angels and Demons:

Ephesians 6:12 (NIV)

For our struggle is not against flesh and blood, but against the rulers, against the authorities, against the powers of this dark world and against the spiritual forces of evil in the heavenly realms.

God created angelic beings. Their job is a military army host of ten thousand times ten thousand more for a heavenly purpose but some rebelled. Angels are guardians of heaven and demons are guardians of evil. Both are subjected to God. Both understand that they must submit to God's authority and be prostrate to worship God when they see Him (Luke 10:17).

Angels:

Greek: *Aggelos*: messenger. Hebrew: *mal'akh*: messenger | Angels are supernatural messengers created by God to serve and communicate His purpose. God's secret agents, usually not seen or heard unless revealed for an urgent purpose ascending and descending from Heaven. Angels are not to be worshiped; they are helpers. Just like an army, there are different classifications of angels. All are to serve to protect the Kingdom of God and those who belong to the Kingdom (Hebrews 1:14). Seraphim and cherubim are the angels who praise and worship around God's throne and guard it. Archangels are the warriors and messengers who help in performing miracles and facilitate judgment. As a child of God, it is our responsibility to give our ministering angels that are attached to our life, direction to operate on our behalf.

Demons:

Greek: *daimónion*: a fallen angel, heathen messenger, evil spirit. Demons are one-third of the fallen angels who rebelled against God and were cast out of heaven because they followed the evil cherubim Lucifer who despised God. They are Satan's, whose name means "accuser" or "slanderer"; they are committed to Satan's plan to thwart the plans of God. Their mission is to completely annihilate the children of God. They are the "rulers, principalities and powers" against which we must "wrestle" (Ephesians 6:12), but God always win.

Paul wrote this to the church in Ephesus while in prison. He was surrounded by Roman guards receiving the revelation that this is a spiritual war, and we are a part of the Kingdom of heaven's army. As holy vessels for the Lord, we need to protect ourselves from mob attacks that come from evil orders just as the great Roman army suited up for battle. We too must suit up for daily battles as we continue to make great strides toward the goal that we are called to finish.

- **Stand** – This is a military preparation for the battle, unmoved at your post, ready for the next assault - to plant our feet firmly on the rock, being "steadfast and unmovable" (1 Corinthians 15:58).

- **Belt of Truth** – The Gospel truth of Jesus who is the truth, we are to gird ourselves with this belt of truth around our bellies against all false religion and traditions sent to deceive. Out of our bellies flow rivers of living water (John 7:38).

- **Breastplate of Righteousness** – Truth and righteousness are inseparable. God's method of living a holy life of integrity. Breastplates guard your heart because everything flows from it (Proverbs 4:23).

- **Shoes of peace** – Peace of God, ready for their journey to proclaim peace and goodwill that the Gospel is a peace-bringing power in the midst of battle.

- **Shield of Faith** – Over all the rest of the armor, faith is evidence of things unseen, believe past obstacles. It is your faith that says "yes" when everyone says "no." Your faith to believe God is able; extinguished the fiery darts of the enemy.

- **Helmet of Salvation** – protection for our head, thoughts of our minds, strategies, ideas, vision. We take captive every thought to make it obedient to Christ (2 Corinthians 10:5).

- **Sword of the Spirit** – The Word of God. The sword is the words we speak from the Bible. Jesus uses the Word of God to fight off the devil's temptations in the wilderness (Matthew 4:1-11) – An ability to quote the Word of God, to counter the attack at the proper occasions. Times of temptation and trial, the Word will fight back the powers of darkness. Hebrews 4:12: "The word of God is living and powerful, and sharper than any two-edged sword." 1 edge) *Logos*: the word spoken; you hear the word for what it is, logic. 2 edge) *Rhema*: the word goes deeper and penetrates the heart for immediate action of utterance for transformation.

- **Pray in the Spirit** – Spirit-filled prayer or speaking in tongues – strong and incessant petitions or pleadings, till the evil is averted, or the good communicated in supplication for ourselves, and in the form of intercession for others.

Philippians 4:8 (NIV)

*Finally, brothers and sisters, whatever is true, whatever is noble, whatever is right, whatever is pure, whatever is lovely, whatever is admirable--if anything is excellent or praiseworthy--***THINK** *about such things.*

Dr. Caroline Leaf, a certified neurosurgeon, has great biblical teaching with scientific evidence of our brain and how everything in our life is manifested by the thoughts in our minds. When we look under a microscope, our nerve endings look similar to trees. We have toxic thoughts that look like dead trees and good thoughts that look like blossoming trees of life. We can change our brains, our thoughts, and our minds. Your brain is constantly functioning even when you are asleep. The activity of our brain does not stop. Our brain is wired for love and to think positive thoughts for our lives to prosper healthily. When we think negative thoughts of anger, bitterness, lust, and all these things our nerve endings in our brain become distorted and our body physically breaks down and responds as if our body is in trauma, then it tries to repair itself. We have free will and control over our lives. Through our thinking our genes can change. Biblical truth says we are made in His image (Genesis 1:27) and we have the mind of Christ (1 Corinthians 2:16). The Bible instructs us to think happy thoughts. When we meditate on the Word of God, we choose to think about what is good. We think of our choices in what we believe. Whatever we do is because we made a choice to do it, think on it, and act on it. Our choices have consequences. We have to be accountable for our actions. Our choices to do either good or bad are the choices of our free will. What we feed our minds will influence our decisions. Our body is controlled by our soul and our soul is controlled by a spirit. When you accepted Jesus, the Holy Spirit that lives inside you helps guide you into transforming into the character, image, and likeness of God. With our minds, we decide to read, memorize, learn to know the Word of God. It is when our mind chooses to apply God's promises to our life. Our thoughts are decisions of choice, what we choose is what we allow. We must make sure the choices we make align with the Word of God. We align with God by studying the Word of God day and night, through prayer; we are to think on all these things. For God has not given us a spirit of fear and timidity, but of power, love, and (sound mind) self-discipline/control (2 Timothy 1:7). Our negative thoughts are strongholds; we must pull down the bad thoughts. Every 21 days recycle your thoughts to think whatever is true, whatever is noble, whatever is right, whatever is pure, whatever is lovely, whatever is admirable, anything that is excellent or praiseworthy. We rebuild and reverse the nerve endings into healthy molecules connected to our DNA that was damaged from negative thinking in our brains, our health improved by the decisions of our minds. Put our focus on God, RENEW our minds for our wisdom, knowledge, and understanding to align with God for our whole life to prosper. Take your thoughts in your mind, put them in your hands, and give them to the Holy Spirit and ask God, "Show me your way, truth, and life" to help you make the right decisions.

Psalm 119:71

It was good for me to be afflicted so that I might learn your decrees.

There is value in what God allows to happen. God uses hardships to shape our hearts, test our motives, and humble our hearts in the lessons that are necessary to bring out our maturity. A new direction that would have never happened if we did not go through these hardships. Going THROUGH one side of something means you have to reach the end of what we are passing through. This moment in time is not permanent because it is a season that has to pass. There is a blessing on the other side waiting for us. The afflictions we face are followed by promotion. The trials are a sign of a breakthrough that is coming. These are just seasons of your life, and seasons change.

There are times of laughter and times of sadness. One who is blessed has suffered a few things. Jesus said people will speak against you saying "all kinds of evil" about you for His namesake. He did not say blessed are you who are wealthy, have a high-ranking status or have fancy cars. Those are just perks. God's abundance was not placed on earth to satisfy our fleshly desires, but rather, to establish the Kingdom of God. God can take the perks away to test our hearts and we will still be blessed. We can tell how blessed we are by our storms. The bigger the storm, the bigger the blessing. We are blessed to be a blessing to others (Zechariah 8:13).

Philippians 4:12 (NIV)

I know what it is to be in need, and I know what it is to have plenty. I have learned the secret of being content in any and every situation, whether well fed or hungry, whether living in plenty or in want.

God is a sovereign God, which means He possesses supreme or ultimate power to rule. God has the authority and has the right to stop your personal plans. God's planned will and purpose for our lives are to stay on the right track He prepared for us. If God allows hardship, it is going to bless us. God is with us through the whole situation. We are not alone. The devil is a liar who tries to make us think we are alone, saying, "God doesn't love you." God does love us; God is love. The things we go through are for growth, to multiply, and take dominion. The devil's lies are ways to lure us into disunity, detach, and separate us from God so our hearts become bitter and angry (Titus 3:9-11). Again, the devil lies, steals, kills, and destroys, in that order, but God is always ahead of the devil on everything. Meaning God always has a plan prepared for every circumstance and already knows what will happen before the events occur. During our time of affliction, God will reveal who is for us and who is against us. Do not get discouraged when God reveals people's true characteristics. God will open our eyes to see what is safe around us and what is not safe. Where we fail is when we keep giving people the benefit of the doubt, with high hopes they will change or the excuses we make for their behaviors instead of confronting the issue. We cannot keep sweeping things under the rug and call the room clean. I have watched leaders reward horrible behaviors to prove their favoritism or alliance. God shows no favoritism (Acts 10:34). The Word says those who operate in favoritism are unlawful because it's a sin (James 2:8-9). Why is favoritism a sin? Favoritism or partiality is a mirror of our ego or image. One word means "to resemble," and the other word means "taking side with." It literally means, "to take hold of a person's face." Favoritism causes us to make judgments about people based on their appearance or image, it will not matter how loyal one is toward another. We are to love our neighbors, not idolize certain people for our benefit to fit an outward image and reject the rest. God will take the veil off our eyes and show us anyone operating in darkness and expose the motives of their hearts and bad behaviors. Do not be weary in well-doing (Galatians 6:9). God has to weed out the red flag things, red flag people, and even the red flag locations. We might end up in places that feel unknown, but that is part of the plan of God for us to rely totally on Him.

1 Corinthians 10:10-11 (NIV)

And do not grumble, as some of them did—and were killed by the destroying angel.

These things happened to them as examples and were written down as warnings for us, on whom the culmination of the ages has come.

Whatever is blocking us has to go. Be careful of the words of our mouth. Do not grumble, do not complain because you are blocking your blessings. Your blessing is being killed by a destroying angel sent to snatch your blessing (Mark 4:1-20).

Affliction drives us to humility. The sincerity of our core values and greater insight on God's decree are postures of our hearts to better trust in God. God looked at a lump of coal and said let's put it through the most intense pressure to become a diamond. That is the same thing in our lives. He saw our coal life and said nope this person is a diamond, let's put this person under intense pressure to make them the most precious jewel. The problem is when people in your life interrupt the process, step in and block the lessons we are supposed to learn. Family and close friends who are overprotective do not let their children get scraped knees. If they do not get hurt once in a while, they lose normal lessons and have to go through lessons the hard way because the people they know step in to block it, not just their lessons, but their blessing of life's adventures. It is dangerous to step into other people's battles or intentionally block other people's blessings. Caterpillars do not know they will become a butterfly. At the right season, the caterpillar makes itself a cocoon. Cocoons will endure rain, heat, wind, and all kinds of weather conditions while protecting the caterpillar's transition into a butterfly. Interruption in the development of the cocoon will prematurely stop the transition process. The butterfly cannot fly if it does not fully develop its wings if the cocoon was broken open too soon. The whole process must happen to become a butterfly that can fly. It is dangerous to interrupt someone's development. They have to scrape their knees to see what life has to offer them. Otherwise, they will be stuck and can't fly on their own. Learn to thank God because your development process taught you how to fly or turned you into a diamond. The greater the affliction, the greater the blessing.

Trust in God

Micah 7:5-6 (AMP)

Do not trust in a neighbor [because of the moral corruption in the land];
Do not have confidence in a friend.
Guard the doors of your mouth
From her who lies in your bosom.
For the son dishonors the father and treats him contemptuously,
The daughter rises up [in hostility] against her mother,
The daughter-in-law against her mother-in-law—
A man's enemies are the men (members) of his own household.

When we are vulnerable, evil spirits use people to operate in lies, betrayal, manipulation, abuse boundaries, and all kinds of division. These are setups to divert our vision or our mission to get us to operate in the lust of the flesh, the lust of the eyes, and the pride of life. For instance, when we sit on a chair, we do not think about anything except that we trust that the chair will hold us up and not fall apart. The moment we sit on the chair and hear a little crack we get up and tell people not to sit on that chair because it is unstable. For some reason, we keep the chair anyway. At some point, we plan on fixing the chair because we like it. Then time passes and we let our guard down, forgetting the chair was unstable. We grab the unstable chair, sit on it, it breaks, then obviously we fall on the floor. We toss that chair out and get a new chair that is sturdy. It is the same with people, addictions, a job, or your living situation. We reach a breaking point. Sometimes you keep the unstable chair too long and eventually our trust breaks into a million pieces before we toss it out. God says in Micah 7:5 not to trust in people, be careful to whom you speak. At some point, we put our guard down and let people who are not obedient to God influence us in the wrong direction (1 Kings 12:1-24). We spoke to the wrong people, we trusted in their false love, protection, and guidance, and ended up doing the opposite of what God advised us to do. God says to guard our hearts, for everything we do flows from it (Proverbs 4:23). Sometimes we must guard our next moves and not tell anyone what we are doing (Mark 7:36). We always have to be on guard for counterattacks and theft on the blessing. The moment we drop our guard is when the devil comes in with attacks from the people closest to us with a mission to stop what God is building within our hearts. Some people want us blessed and want us to succeed, but not more than them. They watch us closely for the moment we do something revolutionary. As we start making a move, here comes adversity pushing us out the way. They take our ideas for themselves to say as loudly as they can, "Look, I did this," to drown out any credit toward us. But God says trust me and I'll show you mysteries and hidden treasure that no one knows during these dark times (Jeremiah 33:3, Isaiah 45:3). God says let them have their fake glory they created for themselves, do not react, do not retaliate, just be still. God says, "Leave your country, your kindred, and your father's household, and go to the land I will show you. I will make you into a great nation, and I will bless you; I will make your name great so that you will be a blessing. I will bless those who bless you and curse those who curse you; and all the families of the earth will be blessed through you" (Genesis 12:1-3). Sometimes we might have to leave the place we serve because the place we serve does not value or honor the blueprint vision that God gave us. Some people want to steal the vision and have you serve under oppression. God will lead you out to a place that He shows you that you will be able to serve with the gifts He imparted to you with honor so you can prosper rather than being used as a pawn.

Do not fear because God is with you. Your victory is found when you trust in God alone. There is no fear or worry, we know God is going to come through. The victory is already won, and God will lead you on the path toward the finish line. Trust God.

Exodus 23:22 (NIV)

If you listen carefully to what he says and do all that I say, I will be an enemy to your enemies and will oppose those who oppose you.

This is a miracle to get the promise back. I love the story of these two women in the Bible (2 Kings 4:1-37). One was a widow and a single mom struggling financially with two boys. Her husband loved the Lord, who was her security covering, had died. Then other was a Shunammite woman who was given a secret desire of her heart to have a son, who ends up dying. Two deaths, one of provision and the other of promise. The widow goes to the prophet Elisha and says my provision is dead, and he told the widow to take her resources in her home which was overflowing oil in jars, and multiply it. He helped her discover she was an entrepreneur with the oil she had in her house. The widow was able to pay her debts and financially support her family by selling the oil. The Shunammite woman was rich but she lacked one thing, a child. She showed great honor toward the man of God (Elisha). God blessed her with a son as her reward even though she didn't ask or pray for a son. Yes, God sometimes gives you desires or blessings of responsibility you do not ask for. Well, her son ends up dying. The promise that God gave her died. If you read the story carefully, you will see that she was emotionally detached from her promise until her son died of neglect and dehydration. She runs to the man of God saying you gave me this promise, now it's dead, and you can bring it back to life. Elisha brings the boy back to life, and the woman can embrace the son. The promise was for her to embrace a son. God had to teach her to care for and embrace her promise. Some things have to die for something new to grow in its place. So many people secretly struggle in their journey, in their call, and definitely in the ministry. Even though they are in great distress they walk around saying everything is all right. Sometimes we must worship God where we are in spirit and in truth during transition seasons. If we read the whole story of the Shunammite woman, she went through ups and downs saying, "I'm all right." Her example of the capacity for empathy, her ability to grow spiritually and facilitate the spiritual growth of others, her willingness to be proactive, and her humility are all qualities that God desires in us in all of our seasons. Do not ever judge people. No one knows what people are going through. So many times, people make great strides in the Lord and get greatly attacked for being obedient. They are given great responsibilities they did not ask for and have to navigate and learn how to adjust to this new thing. As they walk this journey alone, darts are coming at them on every side, they have to press toward the finish line. God is fighting your battles. God sees every single thing. Everything is going to be all right.

Matthew 5:44 (NKJV)

But I say to you, love your enemies, bless those who curse you, do good to those who hate you, and pray for those who spitefully use you and persecute you.

Do you go through a cycle of only allowing people in your life who flatter you, boost your ego, and you can control? Your friends are not your fan club, and some of your fan club attendees need to get kicked out of your VIP section. We have to let real friends tell us the truth to keep us grounded in our lives even if we do not like what they have to say but we know we need to hear the truth we do not want to expose. True friends will tell us the truth because they love us and they express their concerns with compassion, not in judgment or shame. We are more than willing to "keep it real" with other people but when people are real with us, we kill them off, replacing them with someone else whom we want to agree with and participate in our disobedience. Don't purposely try to find faults, accusations, twisted lies, ridiculous high demands, and unrealistic expectations in people as a setup against those who are sent to keep us grounded as an excuse to kill them off. Instead of facing our truth, which makes us uncomfortable, we beat people down and expect them to be loving so we point our finger at them going, "Look what they did to me!" That is manipulation, which is a form of witchcraft.

People are not sent to worship our egos, or finance our poor decisions, pay our life debt, or be placed in a category that blames someone else for the mess we caused. People are sent to pray and cover together. We tend to murder genuine friendships that were supposed to be a covering and lasting friendship for each other because we do not want to face our broken reality. The ruin of a friendship happens when one gets offended, they would rather protect their vanity, not face ownership of their drama than face the reality of the truth. Some friends were given the blessing of grace and compassion, to be honest, and help us, not hurt ourselves. Stop covering up what we do not want people to see because we are afraid of being exposed and losing control. We cover our mess up with humor, material things, or the superficial images we present to everyone that we got it all together to build our ego to protect what we externally portray. It is possible if we do not correct our heart and repent, we become wicked in enjoying other people's failures, being defensive, and accusing other people that have only been nothing but gracious to help us. Do not get an attitude or point the finger when people whom God sent to you as a blessing have had enough of your antics and leave. If you fail to accept the truth, then you fail in trust. Without truth, there is no trust. If you have trust issues, you will never accept the truth.

Some people are gifted in taking the wicked veils off of people's eyes, not to harm but to help each other. James 5:16 said, "Therefore **confess** your sins to each other and **pray** for **each other** so that you may be **healed**. The prayer of a righteous person is **powerful** and **effective**." Exposure is to build each other up, not tear each other down. We are instructed to pray for one another because when two or more agree in prayer it is powerful and effective (Matthew 18:19). It takes a strong person to love people enough to be a prayer covering even though they have been rejected. That is a true friend and true love despite someone's disrespect. Some people do this to God. When God exposes things about ourselves for the purpose of repentance, we get offended. We reject God because we do not want to face our truth that we are out of order. We believe what we want to believe, not what God said. God gives us opportunities to correct our wrongs, loving us despite our disrespect and rebellion. When we face the truth, truthfulness leads us to repentance. Once we repent, we experience freedom from our sins. The goal is unity, not discord.

Ephesians 4:27

...Do not give the devil a foothold...

God never meant for us to become like the world, that is why we were rejected so we would not fall under the influence of evil. The world was created to become like God's character image and likeness, But the world refuses God's conduct. God will use us to minister to our family and our haters, too. Love your enemies but do not give attention to anything that may cause resentment or irritation. Do not play into sarcasm because sarcasm comes from a root of bitterness. We have the right to separate ourselves from the people who are entertained by disunity. Sometimes God allows rejection because our loyalty was hindering God's call for us to move to the place God wanted us to go. God will allow us to walk through the fire, knowing we are not going to get burnt. God is our vindicator in His time (1 Peter 4:12-19). Rejection is for redirection and protection for something better.

Matthew 16:19

And I will give to you the keys of the kingdom of heaven: and whatever you shall bind on earth shall be bound in heaven: and whatever you shall loose on earth shall be loosed in heaven.

When we pray, we are calling what is on earth to reflect the Kingdom of heaven. God gives us authority to call things into being that has not yet happened. God also gives us authority and dominion to bind and loose as we share the good news of Jesus throughout the world. When we are binding and loosing things, we are saying what we allow and disallow or to prohibit and to permit. Binding and loosing were terms frequently used among the Jews that meant bidding and forbidding, granting and refusing, declaring lawful or unlawful. There was a woman in the Bible who had been crippled by a spirit for eighteen years. Jesus said to her, "Woman, you are loosed from your infirmity" (Luke 13:12). Sinners are tied and bound with the chain of their sins. "To bind" is to forbid, to pronounce unlawful; "to loose" is to allow, to declare lawful. When we pray against opposition or in intercession, we call out what is coming against us like this: "I come against and bind every evil spirit coming against me and command that unclean spirit to be loosed off my life. In Jesus's name, Amen."

John 8:32

"Then you will know the truth, and the truth will set you free."

Freedom declaration: Speak the truth with our words and declare the name of Jesus.

God says that we have the power within us to declare victory. We speak prosperity in our lives. The veil is taken off of people's eyes and everyone will see that we are called to work great exploits for the Kingdom. God is opening up the windows of heaven pouring down a blessing so great we will not have room enough to receive it. God is our healer. God is our Savior. God is our deliverer. We are taking dominion; we will give and not borrow. We are the head and not the tail, above and not beneath. We are blessed going in any situation and blessed coming out of all situations. We carry generational destiny going forth with innovation and creativity where God wants us to be. We are filled with fire from the Holy Ghost to take dominion to cast out demonic spirits. Stepping into new and greater callings, the works of our hands are prosperous with great power and authority. Those who are in the pit are climbing out. Those who were forgotten will be remembered. Those who were depressed will rejoice. Those who were rejected will be accepted. Those whose heads were low will lift their heads high. Those who grieve will have laughter. Those who are poor will say they are rich. We will not be crippled by confusion. We will not settle in mediocrity. Those who feel behind will accelerate. Those who experience defeat will experience the greatest victory of their lives. We are magnets for miracles. What was hard will be easy. What was shattered will be restored. Those who were afflicted will be comforted. Those who are sick will be healed. God will restore us completely; whatever the devil stole from us has to be put back sevenfold, that means with interest. What was meant for evil God is turning it around for our good. There are wide open doors of opportunity that we are stepping into that no man can shut. Everything coming against us has to ricochet and go back to the sender. God's love is putting all the broken pieces back together again, blessing us so we can become a blessing to others. We are covered by the blood of Jesus. Praise God and thank Him for a new beginning. Thank Him for the new blessings. Thank Him for the new life. Thank Him for the increase. All in the name of Jesus the Christ of Nazareth.

Psalm 119:11, 105 (NIV)

I have hidden your word in my heart
that I might not sin against you.
Your word is a lamp for my feet,
a light on my path.

CHAPTER 13
PROPHETIC VS SPIRIT OF DIVINATION

Matthew 24:24

For false Christs and false prophets will appear and perform great signs and wonders that would deceive even the elect, if that were possible.

There are two spiritual realms operating on earth, the Holy Spirit and evil spirits. Both are operating in supernatural functions. Most teachers do not teach spiritual warfare. They teach the goodness of God and the Gospels but forget to equip people on recognizing the fruit of evil. We get saints who fall into backsliding traps because they were not taught spiritual warfare or casting out demons. People are not able to pinpoint the root of an evil spirit in a person, instead slap on a worldly title and call it "mental illness" instead of a murder or "sexual orientation" instead of perversion or confusion.

The Holy Spirit is omnipresent, operates in truth and all power, and has the authority to function freely to take dominion of territories bringing order for the Kingdom of God. The evil spirit cannot be in many places at once. Since evil spirits have limited power and cannot have the authority to function as the Holy Spirit, they operate in groups to overtake areas. They are counterfeit operations in unauthorized territories for chaos and disorder. The enemy wants to keep us quiet because our authority is activated when we speak words of truth by the Holy Spirit.

Matthew 23:15 (NIV)

"Woe to you, teachers of the law and Pharisees, you hypocrites! You travel over land and sea to win a single convert, and when you have succeeded, you make them twice as much a child of hell as you are.

Children of God are filled (saturated) with the Holy Spirit. That means evil spirits cannot enter into a Holy Spirit filled believer, once a believer is baptized in the Holy Ghost and the Holy Spirit takes residence inside of a person. Every unclean spirit gets evicted. Every holy thing cannot reside with evil, only cleanliness. God's holiness will take its reign and rule where purity resides. If a person is filled with evil spirits, that is an indication that they have not been baptized in the Holy Spirit and they have allowed unclean spirits to reside in them to operate. Evil spirits look for people to reside in that they can devour. The devil does not show any respect for you, your family, or your household, especially if you are a child of God. Any evil spirit will subtly use every avenue it can, such as drugs, alcohol, sex, money, and power to control a person, distorting their character and keep them in a place where they are bound by evil and destroying everything good in their life.

Mark 5:2-13 (AMP)

When Jesus got out of the boat, immediately a man from the tombs with an ***unclean spirit*** *met Him, and the man* ***lived in the tombs****, and* ***no one could bind*** *him anymore, not even with chains. For he had often been* ***bound with shackles [for the feet] and with chains****, and he tore apart the chains and broke the shackles into pieces, and* ***no one was strong enough to subdue and tame him****. Night and day he was* ***constantly screaming and shrieking*** *among the tombs and on the mountains, and* ***cutting himself with [sharp] stones****.*

Seeing Jesus from a distance, he ***ran up and bowed down before Him [in homage, honor or respect]****; and* ***screaming with a loud voice****, he said, "What business do we have in common with each other, Jesus, Son of the Most High God? I implore you by God [swear to me], do not torment me!" For Jesus had been saying to him,* ***"Come out of the man, you unclean spirit!"*** *Jesus was asking him, "What is your name?" And he replied,* ***"My name is Legion; [for we are many demons residing in him]."*** *And he began begging Him repeatedly not to send them out of* *the region. Now there was a large herd of pigs grazing there on the mountain. And the demons begged Him, saying, "Send us to the pigs so that we may go into them!"* ***Jesus gave them permission.*** *And the* ***unclean spirits came out [of the man] and entered the pigs****. The herd, numbering about two thousand, rushed down the steep bank into the sea; and they were drowned [one after the other] in the sea.*

It is super important to talk about these things especially in a time where Christianity is being attacked more and more. The reason why I gave this its own chapter is because we will see witchcraft operate in hidden forms. People get easily captivated by supernatural things, opening doors to demonic operations that are trying to normalize what God detests. The news is full of faction. We have young adults and teens turning to the occult never knowing the truth of God but persuaded by current popular delusions. Netflix promotes shows with satanic images of false worship. On social media, people have their yoga chants in labyrinths with gemstones of false healing powers. The most common is the entertainment industry promoting mediums and psychics to name a few. Music, movies, and television have made people so numb to evil incantations that children are now twerking as entertainment on TikTok, and parents have allowed this in their home. A person's future is not determined by the constellation or horoscopes, that is superstition.

Exodus 7:22 (NIV)

But the Egyptian magicians did the same things by their secret arts, and Pharaoh's heart became hard; he would not listen to Moses and Aaron, just as the LORD had said.

The truth in all of this is a counterfeit operation from the doctrine of demons operating in divination. Even some *Christian* churches have operated in the occult with magic feathers and gold dust flying through the air. There is nothing biblical about parlor tricks except that is deception. When Moses and Aaron went up against Pharaoh to save the Israelites from slavery, they came with supernatural power with signs and wonders. The magicians came against Moses and Aaron saying look we can deceive people by doing the same thing. So, God said you cannot deceive death, so God sent the angel of death to kill all the first-born sons of the land. All the first-born sons that were saved were the ones who were covered by the blood of the lamb on their doorpost. There are people following humans calling themselves the "messiah" but there is only ONE Messiah whose blood has all power to save and that is Jesus. Everyone else does a little magic trick, swindles money from people, and then they end up dead or a has-been. Teenagers looking for a thrill playing with the Ouija board. Some people have a collection of crystal rocks for energy healing and chakras. These are all deceptive lies and access doors to evil spirits. What you worship you become.

Genesis 18:20 (NIV)

Then the Lord said, "The outcry against Sodom and Gomorrah is so great and their sin so grievous..."

Every region, city, and neighborhood has a different demonic occupancy. When you come to San Francisco, you are most likely going to encounter a homosexual occupancy. If you go to Philadelphia, you will encounter the occupancy of heroin. Demonic occupancy also is in groups of people who practice lawlessness and disrespect toward authorities for a chaotic outcome. The Holy Spirit gives us discernment so that we are not deceived or captivated by the deception of divination.

Galatians 5:19-21

The acts of the flesh are obvious: sexual immorality, impurity and debauchery; idolatry and witchcraft; hatred, discord, jealousy, fits of rage, selfish ambition, dissensions, factions and envy; drunkenness, orgies, and the like. I warn you, as I did before, that those who live like this will not inherit the kingdom of God.

Galatians mention everything that we see on the news every day. The word witchcraft or sorcery is the Greek word *pharmakeia*, where we get the word pharmacy. It means the use or the administering of drugs, poisoning, sorcery, and magical arts. Rebellion and witchcraft are the most dangerous sins because they work together in manipulation. The spirit of divination operates addictions that come into play with potions, spells, and hexes that you find in drugs, alcohol, and sometimes certain grocery store foods and drinks are linked to groups operating in divination. For example, cocaine was used as medicine and was the first ingredient in Coca-Cola. A few years ago, they had bath salts that had people running around biting people's faces off. They called it the "zombie" drug. When people were interviewed, they said they did not know what happened, and "a voice," told them to do it. Maybe more popular is MDMA "molly/ecstasy" which is a pleasure hallucinogenic. These as well as marijuana and shrooms are used in pagan witchcraft.

When I started ministering on the streets and met people saved from the occult, they shared with me how these things tied together. Most homes that occupy people who are under the demonic bondage of addictions open the door to many other demons for the full destruction of the foundation of the security of their home, the peace of their home, the unity of the family, and any financial protection. Family members enable their loved ones who are addicted need to break free from wicked "soul-ties" (an unhealthy connection that causes people to bond together) of bondage that keeps this destruction continuing. God does not step into chaos, delusion, perversion, and confusion. The demon needs to be cast out and removed entirely for the order of God to be put back into the home and family.

Micah 2:11 (NLT)

Suppose a prophet full of lies would say to you, "I'll preach to you the joys of wine and alcohol!" That's just the kind of prophet you would like!

Divinations operate in nightclubs across the nation. I witnessed this firsthand when I worked in the nightclub scenes, then when I went back to minister in strip clubs it gave me a whole new awareness that I will share with you. Here is just one scenario: A concoction is made by the drug dealers and they test the drug on people. If the person who took the drug did not die from an overdose, they sell it on the streets. The drug dealers go to the club to find naive girls. They are in operation with the bartenders who brew up the strong drinks to get these young girls into a state of hallucinations and intoxicating behavior. Now they gave access to demons to take full control to operate in them. The bartender keeps giving these girls the "fun drinks" with all the colors for their social media posts. The girls go to the dance floor to have a good time. The bartender tips off the drug dealers and or the predators who go to clubs to lace drinks to capture girls "home" to their human trafficking ring and test more drugs on these girls so they can be in a zombie state not knowing where they are and not having control of their bodies. Then you mix this in with demonic or "trance" music from the DJ's playlist who influence demonic, perverted, animal-like behaviors. This cycle operates the highest from the hours of midnight to 3 am, what they call the Devil's Hours or "third watch." Most prayer warriors get woken up for prayer intercession around this time during "fourth watch" which is from 3 am - 6 am. Most deaths happen during this hour.

Isaiah 5:20

Woe to those who call evil good and good evil, who put darkness for light and light for darkness, who put bitter for sweet and sweet for bitter.

We have to understand people who are operating in the occult. Granted their belief is sinister, but they are normal people. They walk their dogs, play soccer, and have picnic family BBQs like you and me. We hear the "occult" you think of the Manson family. It is people whose souls are lost, seeking supernatural answers in fortune-telling, tarot cards, gemstones, hallucinogenic meditations, and all the wrong places with illegal information from demonic forces. It seems fun at first, but they do not understand the danger they're in playing with the demons' mission to kill them. The demons that operate in signs and wonders can be tested.

Prophet Elijah stood on a mountain and challenged the 450 prophets of Baal (a false god) to perform supernatural things. Elijah proposed that two sacrifices should be brought, and the God who would answer the call by sending fire to consume the sacrifice, would be deemed the true God. The god Baal did not answer the prophets and left their sacrifice exposed. Elijah called on the name of the Lord; God then answered by a fire burning the sacrifice and the altar. The 450 prophets saw their sorcery did not work and turned from Baal to worship God (1 Kings 18).

Deliverance ministries recognize spirits and operations they usually call them out by name. Some ministers who operate in deliverance ministries will notice traits that are similar to people in the Bible. Deliverance ministries try to get to the root of the evil by rebuking the issued name (addiction, abuse, and poverty). What you see on the surface might just be the fruit. Evil spirits operate in clusters; we must get to the root. They might associate the function people operate in by the name of people who operated in similar ways. Here is a shortlist of evil people operating in unclean spirits in the Bible for your awareness:

Jezebel (1 Kings 16-22) wife of Ahab

- Aggressive passion for domineering and controlling others, especially in the spiritual realm
- Taunted and ridiculed people's weakness
- Murderous, discord, elimination of the work of the Kingdom of God, hates covenant relationship
- Sexual immorality, idol worship, witchcraft/sorcery

Ahab (1 Kings 16-22) husband of Jezebel

- Passive-aggressive, seeks peace with false humility, coward
- Gives away his authority to Jezebel
- Avoids conflicts but has resentment
- Fear's wrath of Jezebel, people pleaser
    - Jezebel and Ahab go hand in hand. You cannot have one without the other. If there is a Jezebel there is always an Ahab or vice versa.

Absalom (2 Samuel 3:3, 13-19 King David's son) / **Korah** (Numbers 16:1–3)

- Undermines leadership and manipulative with the intention to overthrow
- Competitive and self-centered
- Charming and impressive; use kindness and love against people
- Rebellious

Legions (Mark 5:1–5) military term for an army

- 5,000+ of demons in one person
- Torment, chaos, harassment, cut himself with stones, self-destructive
- Untamable nature, wild person and great strength
- Lived among the tombs of dead people and could not be kept in captivity, wild animal

Leviathan (Job 3:8, Job 40 -41, Psalm 74:14, Psalm 104:26 and Isaiah 27:1) Described like a reptile

- Arrogant, self-exaltation, demand everything of everyone
- Hardened heart, haughty eyes
- A lying tongue, stirs up conflict, doesn't admit mistakes
- Uses gifts and revelation to establish the superiority

Amos 3:7 (NIV)

Surely the Sovereign Lord does nothing
without revealing his plan
to his servants the prophets.

Tongues are signs for unbelievers, but prophecy is for believers. The gift of prophecy is **not** fortune telling, to know when the end of the world is to come, or to hear from our dead grandmother. That is divination. The prophetic gifts are of the Holy Spirit for the church of believers in Christ to express edification, exhortation, and comfort toward their purpose in Jesus. The gift of prophecy is the greatest gift; God says we should desire the gift of prophecy. The prophetic word will always have a strategy and solution as to where you need to be that will cause you to persevere that aligns with the Word of God. However, those who operate in the gift of prophecy are subject to someone who operates in the office of a prophet to keep the prophecy in the proper order to discern seasons, places, and time for the message to be spoken (1 Corinthians 14:22-33). With supernatural things there is an element of danger, we must be careful with the words that we speak into someone's life. Those who operate in the prophetic gifts write down and keep a record of their dreams, visions, insights, visuals, divine encounters, and prophetic words. When these come to pass, they go back to their writings as to when God gave them the vision or word. Some prophetic words come through musicians, singers, and dancers who release the sound from heaven to earth through praise and worship. Perfect examples are Miriam and David in the Bible who operated in this way. Prophets are very disciplined in Kingdom order.

Matthew 23:34

Therefore, I am sending you prophets and wise men and teachers (scribes) of religious law.

Now if you are someone who is discovering your prophetic gift, find someone who operates in the office of a prophet to help guide and teach you what is of God and what is not of God as you develop your gift. Find someone whom you trust in the

Lord because most people who operate in the offices of ministry do not give a lot of room for mistakes because of their strong ability to be articulate the mind and heart of God in defining what is right and what is wrong. Their tolerance is not a bad thing and their reaction is not meant to be in a mean way. They just take God very seriously; they do not play games with God or His Word. Prophets react strongly to any form of injustice, oppression, deception, or dishonesty. Prophets hold this function of the gift to strict standards. Prophets are as open about their failures as they want others to be about theirs. Prophets will ask hard questions to expose and uproot what God has not planted into people's lives. Prophets are seers and announcers of God of hidden things for an individual, group, region, nation, or generation. A prophet also gives spiritual counsel and alert the church to any kind of danger followed by a divine strategy.

Never say "God said…" unless you are 100% sure God said it. There might be a message one feels is from God they need to deliver into people's lives but in reality, it is not from God. What they feel is good intentions or jumping to conclusions. Be very careful with the words you speak; they are either for blessing or cursing (James 3:10). Your good intentions or conclusions might steer someone outside of the will of God. It is very dangerous to steer, block, or hinder anyone outside of the will of God. If what is spoken is not of God it can do great damage later either to you, them, or both, although at the time it seemed like the right thing to say. The wisest thing we can do is get connected with a mentor or school that operates in the fruits of the spirit when it comes to our development on any prophetic gifts. Perfect examples are Samuel being under the guidance of Eli (1 Samuel 3); Elisha being under the guidance of Elijah (1 Kings 19 - 2 Kings 2); Ahithophel mentoring Nathan and David (2 Samuel 11-17); Samuel mentored David, too (1 Samuel 16-25). Daniel mentored the three Hebrew boys

(Daniel 3-6). Jesus mentored the twelve disciples (Matthew, Mark, Luke, and John). All these prophetic men went through training.

The **"office of a prophet"** also known as a "seer" will create the future through a revelation of God's will by speaking into existence the answer to the questions as to why God is allowing things to happen by declaring God's Word into someone's life. They will expose hidden gifts, callings, direction, correction, and sin WITH a plan of restoration AND purpose. It can be quite detailed. The **"gift of prophecy"** sees the purpose, gives a confirming word of motivation, insight, and encouragement toward their call.

A prophetic word is a supernatural utterance of inspiration under the power of the Holy Spirit without tongues and interpretation; they are hidden treasures of God to strengthen or build up another. These words will always align with the Word of God. The Holy Spirit flows from the inside out. "Whoever believes in me, as Scripture has said, rivers of living water will flow from within them" (John 7:38).

What is not in order, is someone trying to speak things into existence that are of the world that is detestable to God, that is fortune-telling. For instance, someone tells you that you will die in two months if you don't do x, y, or z. That is a demonic spirit, and you must rebuke it or cast out the evil spirit. The prophetic gift of the Holy Spirit is not for rebuking, opinion, assumption, or criticism. This action can result in their taking the words and actions of the accused out of context to prove their points. The prophetic gift is encouraging the individual or church to prepare them for the Kingdom's work. However, there is a high chance that a prophet will identify the root of a problem for deliverance, a call to repentance. The prophetic word should not come with bitter religion or condemnation. It is possible your flesh that is holding onto sin will get extremely offended or fearful because a prophet will say what you do not want to be exposed to. Understand that accountability feels like an attack when you are not ready to acknowledge your behaviors or habits, especially if they're hidden. The prophetic word is for edification that aligns with the Word of God. If you are living in a harmful way and a prophetic word confirms with the call to repentance, the prophetic word will follow a promise of love and goodness according to the edifying Word of God.

The words will exhort up to keep pressing forward in our Kingdom assignments. A crisis is a gateway and opportunity for prophetic people. God will give a solution to every crisis. Some people come to church broken, exhausted from life, and even suicidal. The prophetic gift will always speak hope back into a person's life with the tenderness and mercy that God gives to function. They think, "My life is over," but God speaks through the prophetic word and says, "No, actually, you have a life and purpose beyond your wildest imagination, and it is good." God does not confuse people but will bring a word of peace to an individual or church. God's message will always come to pass. It might take time, but the word will come into existence. Ask God for the interpretation. We cannot interpret tongues, visions, and dreams in the natural, but we pray and ask God for these gifts. God can give us revelation, mysteries, and insight as to the meaning of a dream and tongues (Daniel 2). The voice of God is clear. Those who are prophetic will discern and sense the hovering heaviness of the Holy Spirit days in advance before communicating God's word (Jeremiah 20:9). You cannot manipulate what you want to hear and what you don't want to hear. God is always speaking; it is always the truth.

Acts 2:17-18 (NIV)

"In the last days, God says,
I will pour out my Spirit on all people.
Your sons and daughters will prophesy,
your young men will see visions,
your old men will dream dreams.
Even on my servants, both men and women,
I will pour out my Spirit in those days,
and they will prophesy."

Now we are calling things that are not and speak to our mountain to be removed (Mark 11:23). Let the poor say I am rich (1 Samuel 2:7). That mountain of poverty needs to go. Let the weak say I am strong (Joel 3:10, 2 Corinthians 12:10). That mountain of weakness needs to go. I know this sounds weird and crazy, but it works. The words out of our mouth have the power of life and death, so speak life and prophecy into every situation. Sometimes God has to see our actions, not just the nice thought in our mind of wishful thinking to know that we are serious. I had gotten to a point that I had to learn how to pray and prophecy to myself.

Some people misuse and manipulate the supernatural weight of the "God said." God speaks, He speaks through the Word of God. Someone says, "God told me." Do those words align with the Word of God? Can you find it in the Bible? You cannot listen to every voice because "God said." God cannot be mocked. God's Word cannot be altered. If it was God, it will at some point come to pass. Same with a vision. Does the vision have a biblical word to back it up? With anything supernatural, get alone with God and pray about the messages given to you, ask God for confirmation through His Word.

Mark 11:23 (NIV)

Truly I tell you, if anyone says to this mountain, 'Go, throw yourself into the sea,' and does not doubt in their heart but believes that what they say will happen, it will be done for them.

Let's speak God's promises over our situations and tell mountains to move. God gave you a voice to have authority over your situation. You read the Word of God, so you speak the Word of God to get in agreement with God to possess the truth and the promises of God. Life and death are in the power of our tongue. Let's speak life. I was a single mom in a serious financial struggle. I was a faithful tither, but something seemed stuck, so I grabbed my ATM card one day, put my hand over it, and spoke Malachi 3:10-12 and called it rich. Money is a tool in the earthly kingdom. In heaven, you do not need money. Today you do. So, take your ATM card, put your hand over it, and command it to submit to God's divine authority. When you submit something under God's authority, it has to follow God's rules. When it comes to money, the rule is giving in tithe and offering that belongs to God. He gets the 10% you get 90%. You must give to receive. It is the principle of sowing and reaping. You cannot do one without the other. God is not a gene in a bottle, He is God. If you are sick, place your hand over that mountain of sickness, speak a verse the Bible says on healing and call that area healed. Put your hand over the cancerous area, put your hand on your head if it is mental health. Put your hand over your heart if it is emotions and command every mountain that does not belong in your body to leave because it does not have authority over you.

Laying of hands

2 Timothy 1:6-7

For this reason I remind you to fan into flame the gift of God, which is in you through the laying on of my hands. For the Spirit God gave us does not make us timid, but gives us power, love and self-discipline.

Most people are used to holding hands and praying. The laying of hands is a symbolic and formal method of action used in the church to transfer gifts of the spirit or the ordination of a position from one person to another. When the apostles chose a person to operate in the office of ministry, they laid their hands on their heads along with anointing oil (Acts 6:6). Why their heads? That is where strategies, ideas, thoughts of the mind function. Laying of hands is also done for transferring blessing or inheritance to people (Acts 13:2; Genesis 48:14). The Bible also says to lay hands on their offering (Leviticus 3:2). You can lay hands for the purpose of healing (Acts 28:8). The laying of hands should only be done after prayer and petition are made to God. The purpose is for a means of grace toward the believer affirming the public display of agreement.

1 Timothy 5:22 (NIV)

Do not be hasty in the laying on of hands, and do not share in the sins of others. Keep yourself pure.

You should not lay hands on people or allow people to lay hands on you until you have the authority by the Holy Spirit and a trusted source. For this reason alone, once you touch someone, you are transforming something to them and vice versa. That is also one of the reasons why there is no sex before marriage, it is the law of transfer. Not only is sex in itself subjected to a risk of a sexually transmitted disease and pregnancy but there is a transference of spiritual attachments "soul-ties" as well for you and your child you conceive. A transference also happens with the people you hang around and the things you tolerate in your inner circle. Even with leaders, your association with immoral people can affect the work you do for the Kingdom of God. Do not be deceived: "Bad company corrupts good morals" (1 Corinthians 15:33).

Do not lay hands on anyone who is not ready to carry the weight of the glory that is on you. If you promote someone through the transference of laying of hands and they were not ready to handle the weight of the glory it will be horrendous for them. If you let someone lay hands on you and you don't trust them, you do not trust their ministry, or you feel something is not right. Do not let them touch you. It is the same for you. Do not touch people until you are sure of your deliverance in certain areas, and you are sure of your authority in Christ and the Holy Spirit prompts with a word from the Bible to back up any transference of blessing or promotion, do not do it. You do not want to invite something upon yourself that is not of God. Just say, "God, speak to me." You do not need hands laid upon you if it is not necessary. God will confirm an impartation through His Word or through someone who operates in the prophetic ministry until you get more mature in the laying of hands. You can lay hands on yourself; you trust yourself. Speak the Bible verse to yourself until the Holy Spirit prompts you otherwise. If there is a gift in the ministry you are passionate about, study and learn about it until God says you are ready to operate in that function. No matter what you have to **study, pray, and wait** for God. While you wait, praise God because He will answer you.

Titus 2:11-12 (NIV)

For the grace of God has appeared that offers salvation to all people. It teaches us to say "No" to ungodliness and worldly passions, and to live self-controlled, upright and godly lives in this present age.

CHAPTER 14
OBEDIENCE

John 14:23 (AMP)

Jesus answered, "If anyone [really] loves Me, he will keep(obey) My word (teaching); and My Father will love him, and We will come to him and make Our dwelling place with him.

God relentlessly pursues us and our response of devotion toward Him through our faith, trusting and believing that in His love our promises are secure. Our journey to walk with God is conditional and not about following rules. Every relationship has boundaries that we are responsible to respect. In the mercies of God, we have free choice to respect and obey the relational boundaries of God. God says ***if*** you will obey my commands I will provide. "If" is the key factor it means 'whether or not' or 'in the event that'. 'If' is used 18,174 times in 12 biblical translations. With every command comes a blessing '*whether or not*' '*in the event that*' you choose to say yes to God.

Hebrews 5:8 (AMP)

Although He was a Son [who had never been disobedient to the Father], He learned obedience through what He suffered.

When God speaks to us, the call is a command and not a negotiation or debate. God's command is for our best interest. God does not respond to your pain, excuses, or complaints. God does not call us for popularity; He chose us to be obedient to His call for a Kingdom purpose. Popularity comes and goes with circumstances and seasons of life. There are more blessings in obedience than there are anywhere else based on our reliance on His provisional sustainability when we obey. A wise person will submit themselves to respond to God's command immediately. When we say yes to God, it saves us from so many troubles because we are in God's alignment. In God's alignment, we are protected, provided for, and are safe.

Luke 14:28 (NIV)

Suppose one of you wants to build a tower. Won't you first sit down and estimate the cost to see if you have enough money to complete it?

At the prompting of God's command, always evaluate the cost of your sacrifices even if it means going against the crowd. Do you need to study? Do you need to separate yourself from people? Do you have to change your behavior? Do you have to go to rehab? Do you need to move to another state? Do you have to throw away sinister entertainment? What do you need to do to build God's Kingdom? You might be the key to the salvation of your whole family.

Jesus paid the price on the cross. The disciples paid the price of many persecutions to minister the Gospel of Jesus. Many men and women of God suffered the cost of what it takes for the Kingdom of God. No matter the opposition there is always a reward of miracles of blessing that overflowing comes to you and for you when you step into obedience. We obey because we love God, and our love for God in our servanthood brings us satisfaction (John 14:15). Our obedience is not "good" works. Although the works we do are good, the goal is a divine outcome. We are a chosen generation picked specifically for this time to take dominion. The deeper you go the bigger the warfare, and the bigger warfare, the bigger the blessing. You are a warrior, strong and courageous, and fully equipped for a Kingdom victory. Whether you choose to go deep in Christ or not, God will reward you if you diligently and continually seek Him in all things.

God is not legalism; you have free will and free choice. He will never ask you or force you to do anything outside of your free will. Understand, obedience is the key to everything. Our obedience unlocks doors to rooms we never imagined in our wildest dreams we would be in. Obedience gives us the invitation to sit at tables we never thought we would be invited to sit at. Obedience is our position to submit to God's command and authority as a Kingdom representative here on earth with an eternal reward.

James 1:22

Be doers of the word and not hearers only, deceiving yourselves.

How do you know when God is speaking? God speaks through His words in the Bible. God speaks through prayer. God speaks through dreams and visions. Lastly, God speaks through men and women of God who operate in the authority to speak into our lives such as a pastor or mentor in Christ. God speaks through circumstances and the inner still small voice that some will call either intuition or conscience. We must be alert in our discernment of what God is saying. Whatever God is saying there will always be a confirmation by His Word to back it up. If you are not sure of the message and if the message is from God, we are authorized to test the spirit (1 John 4:1-6).

1 Corinthians 3:14 (NIV)

If what has been built survives, the builder will receive a reward.

Building what lasts in Christ is consistent, eternal, and sustainable for success and trustworthiness. Be faithful in the small things. Learning to be faithful and serve behind the scenes is where a character is built. The divine enablement of our faith activates what we cannot do in the natural. God wants every part of us to bless Him, even the imperfect areas. Just as much as we want all of God. God is saying I want you to be a part of me, I want your loyalty to what a good relationship is to be.

God says I love you; I want to bless you and give you a life that is good because I planned our days to be successful together, I chose you for myself. When our obedience is to focus on the truth through a covenant relationship with God, we have the benefits of the enjoyment of true love.

1 Peter 2:15-16

For it is God's will that by doing good you should silence the ignorant talk of foolish people. Live as free people, but do not use your freedom as a cover-up for evil; live as God's slaves.

Whatever you do, do it with integrity. People are in pain and cause pain; misery loves company. Their unfaithful ways will cause our foot to stumble. Unfaithful people are going to try to steer our commitment to God in the opposite direction. The conviction of the heart when tempted to steer our focus is the sign that God is pinpointing the areas of change for His greater glory. Integrity is doing something with honesty and having strong moral principles, doing the right thing even when no one is looking. Letting God fight our battles of opposition instead of taking matters into our own hands. Trusting God, believing, and standing on what is right and just with tenacity and honesty. In our faithfulness, God prepares a reward of promotion out of our obedience to stick to His plan.

Matthew 7:21-23 (NKJV)

"Not everyone who says to Me, 'Lord, Lord,' shall enter the kingdom of heaven, ***but he who does the will of My Father in heaven.*** *Many will say to Me in that day, 'Lord, Lord, have we not prophesied in Your name cast out demons in Your name, and done many wonders in Your name?' And then I will declare to them, 'I never knew you; depart from Me, you who practice lawlessness!"*

Anointing: Takes | Blesses | Breaks | Gives

1 John 2:20 (NIV)

"...But you have an anointing from the Holy One, and all of you know the truth..."

God sees you at the point of your need. You are reading this book because you reached a place of "What now?" When you give God all of yourself, that is when God steps into your situations. Jesus noticed food was in a boy's hand and asked if He could use the two fish and five loaves of bread. The moment this kid let go of his lunch, God took the fish and bread, blessed the food, broke the bread, and gave the fish and bread that multiplied and extended the meal to feed five thousand people, including the boy (Matthew 14:17-22).

God will want the most precious thing we have so he can multiply it. We must release the things we feel we need to hold tight so God can supply the multiplication. When people choose to release something, it opens the gateway for multiplication. If we do not release the precious things that are in our hands, God cannot multiply those precious things to turn them into blessings. Jesus multiplied the little resources this boy had, but the boy had to let go of everything he had and trust God. God is the All-Mighty God. God will supply all of your needs. Jesus said I am the Bread of Life (John 6:25-59 NIV). Jesus is our sustenance that gives us life.

This is a representation of our life. Jesus **took** the bread; Jesus takes us into a molding process to become His chosen vessel. Jesus **blessed** the bread; Jesus starts to bless our life. Jesus **broke** the bread; Jesus starts to prune areas of our life that need to be broken off our lives so new things can grow that are good in their place. Jesus **gave** the bread to the people; this is when

God sends us out on assignment to proclaiming what God has done in our lives, the Gospel good news.

John 10:14 (NIV)

I am the good shepherd; I know my sheep and my sheep know me

We often hear God is our Shepherd and we are His sheep. Sheep need a lot of guidance. One of the ways shepherds protected their sheep was to pour oil on their heads. Animals are subject to little pesky bugs like mites, flies, lice, fleas, and ticks. If the infestation of the bugs were not taken care of, the bugs would crawl in the eyes, nose, and ear canal of the sheep. The bugs burrow in the sheep's ear, nest in the sheep's brain, and eat away at their brains, in their eyes to where the sheep can't see, and their noses that make it hard to breathe. The irritation and pain from the bugs would be so severe the sheep would bang their heads against rocks or hard places to ease their suffering, breaking their skulls. The shepherd would take oil, pour the oil all over the sheep's head and face making the wool slippery so the bugs will slip off. God anointed the heads of His people with the first press of olive oil from an olive tree as a symbolic gesture of blessings as shepherds do unto sheep to solidify the calling on God's chosen people as a spiritual symbolism of protection, and empowerment that is in agreement with the scriptures.

1 Samuel 16:7 (NIV)

But the Lord said to Samuel, "Do not consider his appearance or his height, for I have rejected him. The Lord does not look at the things people look at. People look at the outward appearance, but the Lord looks at the heart."

The anointing oil is not magic oil. When God chose Saul to be king, Saul had all the external qualities: handsome, strong, tall, humble, and sensitive to God's leading. Then he became disobedient to God. Saul's humility was now arrogance, pride, jealousy, envy, and depression. God rejected Saul for his arrogance and disobedience. God removed His presence from Saul and sought someone who was after God's heart, David. When the time came for David to be king, he was a teenager working as a shepherd for his father Jesse and his seven brothers. The prophet Samuel wanted to give Saul another chance and keep him as king. God told Samuel to stop mourning his friend and find a new king. However, since David was a young boy and in a job that was the lowest position, God had to prepare Samuel's heart to receive David. God instructed Samuel to put olive oil in the horn of a ram, when the oil starts to flow that is who is to be the next king. When Samuel got to the house of Jesse, Samuel saw David's seven brothers who were training to be valiant warriors, but the oil would not flow for them. So, Samuel asked if there was another son, Jesse and all seven sons said yes there is, but you don't want him. David's father and brothers had rejected David, but God had other plans. They called for David who was in the field with sheep. As soon as Samuel put the horn of oil above David's head, the oil poured out of the ram's horn, drenching the young boy.

It is God who chooses who to anoint a person to be a Kingdom vessel. Most people whom God chooses are the ones that the world rejects (Psalm 118:22, Matthew 21:42-43). God allows His people to go through separation to be holy or pure used for His Kingdom. God looks at the heart, not the exterior. David wrote the most beautiful songs, psalms, hymns of praise to God when he was alone with the sheep, despite being rejected by his family. David's thanksgiving, praise, and worship is what drew God to say, "this is the king I choose for my people, the one who is after my heart."

Some people get anointed in public (1 Samuel 16:13, 2 Samuel 2:4, 2 Samuel 5:3) and some in private (1 Samuel 9-10). The primary purpose of anointing with the holy anointing oil was to sanctify or consecrate the anointed person, to be set apart as "holy" (Exodus 30:29). Originally, the oil was used exclusively for the priests and the Tabernacle articles, but its use was later extended to include kings of Israel (I Samuel 10:1). The oil was the outward seal covenant of God's presence that would only flow until the oil was placed above the right individual's head.

Psalm 40:2–3 (NIV)

"...He lifted me out of the slimy pit, out of the mud and mire; he set my feet on a rock and gave me a firm place to stand. He put a new song in my mouth, a hymn of praise to our God..."

The olive oil goes through a similar process. The first step is taking the olive from the tree to cleanse the olive. The second step is crushing the olives into a paste. The purpose of crushing is to tear the flesh cells of the olive to facilitate the release of the oil from the vacuoles that turns into a paste. Then separating the oil from the rest of the olive components. This used to be done with presses. The final separation, if needed, happens through gravity. This is called racking the oil for filtration. The oil goes through this crushing, pressing, and separation to be used for multiple purposes.

There are two words for anoint:

Hebrew word: (*mashach*): to smear oil, as consecration | Anoint *mashach* is mostly used in the Old Testament

Greek word: (*chrió*): to smear or rub with oil, someone as divinely authorized (appointed by God) to serve in a sacred office such as consecrating Jesus to the Messianic office, and furnishing him with the necessary powers for its administration, empowering the gifts of the Holy Spirit | Anoint: *chrió* is mostly used in the New Testament

Consecration means: to be set apart; holy, purification, dedicate, the action of making or declaring something, appointing or ordaining someone to a sacred office

Another way a shepherd would train their sheep from wandering is in the breaking of their legs. Sheep tend to wander off and stray if they are not led to follow the flock. When the sheep wander from the flock and the shepherd, they are subject to all kinds of harm, predators, and injuries. The way shepherds had to discipline lambs that would stray was with their rod and staff. The rod was like a club used to defend the flock from predators, the staff was long with a huge hook like a candy cane used to nudge the sheep in the right direction. The rod and the staff were weapons of security and protection for the sheep. The shepherd would use his rod to break the leg of a sheep who needed discipline. The shepherd would bind the break, then take the sheep and carry the sheep on the shepherd's shoulders while the wound healed. Through the healing process, the sheep would learn that the shepherd could be trusted by the actions of the shepherd supplying food, transportation, and protection. Once the wound was completely healed, the sheep's dependency on the shepherd would cause the sheep to stay committed to the shepherd. This is symbolic of the breaking process that happens in our life to get us to where God wants us to be.

Proverbs 13:20 (MSG)

"...Become wise by walking with the wise;
hang out with fools and watch your life fall to pieces..."

Jesus's final instructions were for us to spread the good news of the Kingdom, the Gospel. Jesus chose us and filled us with the Holy Spirit as a gift to be fruitful, multiply, and take dominion as representatives of the Kingdom of God. The anointing has weight. Glory is heavy. Some people struggle with carrying the weight of the anointing. The cost is pricey. The deeper you go; the fewer people stay around you. That happened to Jesus. He had a big crowd of followers when he was healing and ministering things that were easy blessings. As soon as Jesus got deep, closer to the finish line of the cross, all of Jesus's crowd of followers got uncomfortable and left. Jesus even turned to his twelve disciples and asked if they were going to leave, too (John 6). The reward is great. You have to lean on faith not cower back when we get into deep waters. Stay connected to those who are obedient and not fallen to fear.

Psalm 37:23

...steps of a good man are ordered of the Lord...

To be saved, it cost nothing for us. Jesus paid the price for our sins when He shed his blood. The moment we choose to be a disciple (disciplined learner) of Jesus, it takes great sacrifice to serve the Kingdom of God. Many are called but few are chosen (Matthew 22:14). The chosen are the ones who accept the conditions of ministry and complete it. The called are ones who lay the foundation but do not complete the task (Luke 14:29). We must sit down and count the cost. We will go through tests, but we learn from them. The assignment always starts pretty easy, then the test, the pressure, the trials, the mountains, and valleys come. This is the pressing season that pulls out the greatness of God, the anointing, through the hard times. The hardest test is when God tells us not to react when we are being persecuted, although we have every right to defend ourselves. God says be still trusting He fights our battles. Once the test is passed there is a great reward for being obedient.

We are born again, that is one level. Then we are baptized in the Holy Ghost speaking in tongues, that is another level. As soon as we start taking dominion and changing atmospheres with signs, wonders, healing, casting out demons, and deliverance, the world might not want to be in your circle. We are messing with the comfort of their sin. They want to cling to the shenanigans of the world. We are disrupting the enemy's plans to keep people bound in their fleshly behaviors. People will start making assumptions about your life and character. God says no eye has seen and no ear has heard the things God has planned for you (1 Corinthians 2:9). God starts something in you, He will complete it (Philippians 1:6). Persevere and keep going past the pain of your breaking point. The anointing, your greatness is in the pressing. You are pressing out the oil to light the fire of God. You are a light in the darkness (John 1:5). God is your strength (Proverbs 18:10).

Service:

Luke 6:38 (NIV).

"Give and it will be given to you. A good measure, pressed down, shaken together and running over, poured into your lap. For the measure you use, it will be measured to you."

I have had the pleasure of working closely with top doctors, executive heads, ministers, and then under the direction of my mentor. I had the honor to work with amazing leaders who operated with open communication and servant leadership. Jesus demonstrated these qualities very well. We are at our very best when we serve. Serving unveils our talents and gifts. Our goal is to be a light in the world to fulfill the great commission of ministering the Gospel (good news) of Jesus Christ. We break down barriers of view that are difficult and sometimes controversial. Yet God appointed us for such a time like this to do things in a revolutionary way that promotes God's goodness and love. Very few are willing to serve in the church while others are willing to reap the benefits of serving God. The business principles are the same in the church as it is in our job. It's important to not have a division between the people of God and the functions of the church, we were created to flow together. God takes normal people to do abnormal things using their gifts. We can serve by agreeing with the plans of God. If two do similar things but different styles, how much more can things get done beautifully blending the two for the love of God and the love of his people? Spiritual growth in connection with God makes us more aware of the Holy Spirit's operations to make us functional and to be able to serve.

1 Corinthians 12:12

For as the body is one and has many parts, and all the many parts of that one body are one body, so also is Christ.

People leave jobs and ministries for two things: lack of communication or they do not feel valued. Every mentor I had either in the business field or in ministry always edified their team and made their team feel that their work was valuable. They did not show favoritism but expressed that their employees were appreciated, not just to some but to all. When shifts in functions happened those changes were communicated with praise, appreciation, with new duties in other areas of responsibilities. Service is about growth. No one was questioning why someone else was doing their job or trying to compete or left any room for arguments when communication and appreciation were done in peace. The team was one body in unity each fulfilling a function or many functions but operating together. When there is no communication or appreciation every operation will come across as shady. Although that might not be the intention.

James 1:21 (AMP)

So get rid of all uncleanness and all that remains of wickedness, and with a humble spirit receive the word [of God] which is implanted [actually rooted in your heart], which is able to save your souls.

When people are not given duties or their duties are taken away from them without a replacement, they will see their service as not having a purpose in the place where they are supposed to serve; it is possible they might not stay very long. If we do not allow people to serve, we are blocking them from blessing us and blocking ourselves from receiving a blessing from them. Although in the beginning, the flow might not be perfect, give the servers time to develop, make mistakes, learn and outgrow where they are to do other things. They might even surprise us!

If we don't want people to serve because we personally don't like them, we cannot get mad and talk about them when they leave. We just lost a good reward when we push people out. That reputation will reflect on you, not them. Remember people are watching leaders' behaviors. If a leader can treat their team member horribly, other team members will know that their leader can be nasty to them as well. People remember bad things before the good. Give everyone something to do and enforce their value. Everyone is valuable, whether we like them or not; it is not about us, it is about the Kingdom of God. Give honor where honor is due. Value and honor are beautiful things. Although pastors are to be highly respected because God chose them for one of the highest offices in the Kingdom, we have to remember to honor and value the people around us, too, not just the pastor only but love our neighbors as well. We do not treat people like garbage and when leadership walks in the room we become an angel. Then leadership wonders why the other person was so down, or their reactions are a certain way. We have to take ownership of our actions; not pretend we did not say or do anything when leadership was not around. What happens in private will reflect in public.

Luke 14:11 (NIV)

For all those who exalt themselves will be humbled, and those who humble themselves will be exalted."

Get along and serve together. There is a great reward in unity, great power when two or more are in agreement. Honor and value work two ways; they are not one-way streets. Remember Jesus who is the highest in leadership took the position of the lowest servant and washed the disciples' feet. He didn't reap all the honor and say wash my feet (John 13:1-17). No, Jesus honored them in return, served them, and told them you need to do the same for each other. If the Holy Spirit says to forgive, then you forgive. If the Holy Spirit says repent, then you repent. You obey the action immediately that is being told to you, not obey the pride that keeps you doing what you are doing that prompted the Holy Spirit to point out your behaviors then gave you a solution to correct what was asked of you to do by repentance. Do not alter God's intended plans for selfish gain, obey the plan and will of God. The reward comes from obedience, not from pride. Our integrity is rooted in God's heart when God's people operate in unity both publicly and privately. Working together as one body in unison and love accomplishes the impossible together.

1 Peter 3:9 (NIV)

Do not repay evil with evil or insult with insult. On the contrary, repay evil with blessing, because to this you were called so that you may inherit a blessing.

Serve even when it is confusing. The Israelite army had to march around the walls of the city gates of Jericho in silence six times. I am sure people who were watching mocked them and wondered what they were doing. Then the army completed the seventh lap around that wall they blew the trumpet and shouted a roar up into heaven and the walls of Jericho came tumbling down and they took over the city (Joshua 6). Even though the assignment did not make any sense at all, they did it anyway. This is where you have to say, "I do not care what people think, I got a job to do for God and I will complete it." God's Kingdom will come; God's purpose will be done on earth as it is in heaven. Do not give attention to the judgments of people who do not like efforts of your obedience to God. You will do what God called you to do. Keep allowing God to transform you by the renewing of your mind. You will not be defeated.

1 Corinthians 1:10 (NIV)

I appeal to you, brothers and sisters, in the name of our Lord Jesus Christ, that all of you agree with one another in what you say and that there be no divisions among you, but that you be perfectly united in mind and thought.

God has all of our prayers in His hands. He has blessed us with all these little graces leading up to our breakthrough. The moment we complete the assignment He gave us to accomplish is the moment we have broken open the overflow of God. God does not withhold anything good from those who love Him. Obedience and love go together. We cannot have love without trust. God will perfect the promise and bring it to us at the right time. When we don't know what to do, we tend to gravitate to what we know. If we know bad habits with bad people, we will keep going back to those things that are familiar. God has to direct us to move into new things that seem impossible through trust. God will allow rejection and persecution in familiar places so we can go in God's direction, not in the same direction we are used to going. We must let go of the familiar places and obediently submit to God's directional leading.

2 Timothy 2:15

Do your best to present yourself to God as one approved, a worker who does not need to be ashamed and who correctly handles the word of truth.

When the promise looks crazy or impossible and we feel alone in an unfamiliar place. When we get to unfamiliar places we must learn to encourage and pray for ourselves. Do not be embarrassed when God tells us to do the impossible. Where we see fear and impossibilities, that is probably the exact path where God wants us to go. Fear perverts the most precious area of breakthrough. The place where we have the greatest battles and most sensitivity is where God wants us to experience a phenomenal victory, the key to our ministry. We praise Jesus when the storm surrounds us, when fear says, "Don't go that way." Praise draws in God's presence. We have to stand our ground talk back to the storm to say, "Peace, be still..." Keep pressing forward. Obey impossible instruction because nothing is impossible for God. When God gives you an instruction, somewhere in between the command and our obedience something happens that was once impossible becomes a possibility in Christ. Faith activates our promise. Do not surrender to fear. Fear will try to counteract faith. Walk by faith, not by sight (2 Corinthians 5:7) ... The Jordan River did not part until the Israelites stepped into the water (Joshua 3-4). You have to take a leap of faith and step into the waters for your rapids to be pushed aside so you can cross on dry land safely to reach your promised land.

2 Samuel 7:28 (NIV)

Sovereign LORD, you are God! Your covenant is trustworthy, and you have promised these good things to your servant.

We are FULLY convinced that even though we do not see the promise yet, the promise is on the way! God is making a way. God is moving people and placing things in position before we arrive at the proper time. God has to move the things that are blocking and hindering us out the way. God puts us in short resting places in between our journey to sustain us. But we keep going. What God started; He will finish. God is continual. It doesn't stop. You got this far. Now you got to keep going. God is guiding your steps toward the promise He has prepared for you. It's prepared already. Once God does it for you, it will be bigger than you have ever imagined! More abundant than your prayer requests! Trust the course God has you in. You are protected and provided for. You can even brag about how good God has been to you with all the surprises He gives you along the way when you obey the conditions in faith. God will do more than you can ever ask or think!

Deuteronomy 6:5-9 (NIV)

Love the Lord your God with all your heart and with all your soul and with all your strength. These commandments that I give you today are to be on your hearts. Impress them on your children. Talk about them when you sit at home and when you walk along the road, when you lie down and when you get up. Tie them as symbols on your hands and bind them on your foreheads. Write them on the doorframes of your houses and on your gates.

Children are the number one ministry. If you ever get a chance to be a children's ministry teacher, it is the best reward. Teaching your children which way, they should go is the most important command. If you are a parent, sibling, friend, family, or an associate of little children, they are your opportunity to plant a seed or win a harvest for the Kingdom of God by sharing the Gospel of Jesus. Children are precious; their minds are developing. If you are a parent, your child is the most important ministry you have. Raise them to know and apply the

Word of God. When you plant the Word of God into their life, it will never depart from them (Proverbs 22:6). It is our duty no matter what child we come across to encourage them, edify them, love them, and speak positive words in their life. A child needs love more than anything.

Psalm 78:1-4 (NIV)

My people, hear my teaching;
listen to the words of my mouth.
I will open my mouth with a parable;
I will utter hidden things, things from of old—
things we have heard and known,
things our ancestors have told us.
We will not hide them from their descendants;
we will tell the next generation
the praiseworthy deeds of the Lord,
his power, and the wonders he has done.

The moment I realized I was going to have a baby; I made a promise to God I was going to do everything I could to raise my baby to know Him. I would put on worship music and put headphones on my belly. I was praying and speaking what I knew at the time, God's truth to my belly. I did not want to miss an opportunity to share the Gospel with my child before I even knew how to share the Gospel. I would speak as much as I knew. When my daughter was almost two years old, she had a pacifier in her mouth, and was not much of a big talker at the time. I was praying over our meal. She pulled the pacifier out of her mouth and said, "Save souls." She put the pacifier back in her mouth and stared at me as two-year-old stare at adults with innocent curiosity. From that day on after every prayer, we said, "Save souls." Little did I know that God was going to train me up under one of the most influential world-renowned evangelists today, Debra George. I have been winning souls for Jesus ever since. God has allowed me to sow seeds into children, youth, single mothers, strippers, prostitutes, homeless, drug addicts, and gang leaders. My daughter and I did not know we were prophesying soul-winning into our lives if I was not obedient to the principle of Deuteronomy 6:6-7.

Proverbs 22:6 Amplified Bible (AMP)

Train up a child in the way he should go [teaching him to seek God's wisdom and will for his abilities and talents], Even when he is old he will not depart from it.

Children need our time and attention. Just like we need value in our work, children need to know they are valued and loved more than anyone. Pay attention to them, be intentional in speaking the promises of God into their life. Tell them they are a child of the Most High God. They can do impossible things in Christ. Tell them about the love of Christ. Tell them about the blood of Jesus. Tell them of eternal glory. As you learn the promises of God, share your knowledge with your kids. Teach them to pray. My daughter learned the Gospel through communion. At every meal our prayer was this: "Father, thank you for this food; we receive your bread of life and your blood of salvation. We declare Jesus is Lord over our life, Amen. Save Souls." we clapped our hands with a "Yay!!" praise then we ate our food. It was simple and it was practical. As Debra George taught me the practicalities of salvation, I taught my daughter the same. My daughter shared with her friends and teachers the simple salvation prayer, "Jesus, come into my heart, forgive me of my sins and be Lord over my life, save my soul, Amen."

Psalm 127:3

See, children are an heritage of the LORD:
and the fruit of the womb is his reward.

Children are our future; they have a purpose. As parents and adults, it is our responsibility to teach children the Bible. Train and prepare them to be a light in darkness in a world full of wickedness. We train them to live out the Bible and live for Him. Do not let society or culture train our children. The children will continue to trust in God to adulthood and impart the Bible to their children. Treat children with tender mercy as God has treated you with mercy. Children are the greatest reward and the most precious gift. Love them as God loves you. God loves His children, and He blesses them beyond measure.

Matthew 7:24 (NIV)

Therefore everyone who hears these words of mine and puts them into practice is like a wise man who built his house on the rock.

As representatives of the Kingdom of heaven here on earth, we are obedient in our homes, on our jobs, in our day-to-day lives. Our obedience is a lifelong process that strengthens our integrity. Serving and giving unto others as we would like done to ourselves is wise beyond compare. We are worshipers trusting in God in all things, not giving into fear in any way. True obedience comes from the heart accepting the grace and mercy of God that is new every morning. Our obedience to God is an expression of not just trust but the love we have for the Father and one another through the forgiveness that God gives so we give to others as well.

Our faith to believe that even in our obedience, our faith in actions is better than sacrifice because of the trust and love for the Father (1 Samuel 15:22–23).

Genesis 22:18 (NIV)

and through your offspring all nations on earth will be blessed, because you have obeyed me.

CONCLUSION

Isaiah 61:1-11 (NIV)

The Spirit of the Sovereign Lord is on me, because the Lord has anointed me to proclaim good news to the poor. He has sent me to bind up the brokenhearted, to proclaim freedom for the captives and release from darkness for the prisoners, to proclaim the year of the Lord's favor and the day of vengeance of our God, to comfort all who mourn, and provide for those who grieve in Zion— to bestow on them a crown of beauty instead of ashes, the oil of joy instead of mourning, and a garment of praise instead of a spirit of despair. They will be called oaks of righteousness, a planting of the Lord for the display of his splendor. They will rebuild the ancient ruins and restore the places long devastated; they will renew the ruined cities that have been devastated for generations. Strangers will shepherd your flocks; foreigners will work your fields and vineyards. And you will be called priests of the Lord, you will be named ministers of our God. You will feed on the wealth of nations, and in their riches you will boast. Instead of your shame you will receive a double portion, and instead of disgrace you will rejoice in your inheritance. And so, you will inherit a double portion in your land, and everlasting joy will be yours. "For I, the Lord, love justice; I hate robbery and wrongdoing. In my faithfulness I will reward my people and make an everlasting covenant with them. Their descendants will be known among the nations and their offspring among the peoples. All who see them will acknowledge that they are a people the Lord has blessed." I delight greatly in the Lord; my soul rejoices in my God. For he has clothed me with garments of salvation and arrayed me in a robe of his righteousness, as a bridegroom adorns his head like a priest, and as a bride adorns herself with her jewels. For as the soil makes the sprout come up and a garden causes seeds to grow, so the Sovereign Lord will make righteousness and praise spring up before all nations.

When we accepted Christ we accepted all of Him, the divine supernatural deity and human in the flesh, both in one person. Jesus's miraculous birth was from a virgin. The miracles Jesus performed and taught His disciples for a three-year hands-on training. Jesus's beating, suffering, and death on the cross as a living sacrifice debt payment for our sins. Jesus's resurrection was not as a ghost but as a human person alive. "And being found in *appearance* as a man, he humbled himself by becoming *obedient* to death—even death on a cross" (Philippians 2:8, NIV). Then Jesus was for 40 days on earth walking with His people to prepare them for the Holy Spirit. We believe Jesus ascended into heaven and is seated at the right hand of the Father making intercession for us when we pray in His name. Jesus is coming back the same way He left in the clouds. We believe He sent the Holy Spirit to help us continue His work to bring the Kingdom of heaven here on earth until His return.

1 Corinthians 15:14, 20

And if Christ be not risen, then is our preaching vain, and your faith is also vain. But now is Christ risen from the dead and become the firstfruits of them that slept.

Our salvation was granted by the shed blood of Jesus. Our victory is in the fact that Jesus defeated death by rising from the dead. He was walking around with proof of His wounds in His hands and the piercing in His side (John 20:24-29). We now can go directly to God in prayer and ask whatever we want according to His will for our life (1 John 5:14). By faith, we believe that every prayer is answered with a "yes" and "amen" (2 Corinthians 1:20). We know we were created for divine destiny, fashioned by God (Job 33:4, Psalm 119:73). God is guiding us into places of victory and turning around every situation. God is the same yesterday, today, and tomorrow

(Hebrews 13:8). God is the Name above every name (Philippians 2:9). God went ahead of us by day in a pillar of a cloud to guide us on our way, and by night, in a pillar of fire to give us light, so that we could travel safely under His protection in our purpose (Exodus 13:21). God is the one who makes us prosper in the time of famine (Psalm 37:19). Yahweh is God's name (Exodus 3:13-15). God is from everlasting to everlasting (Isaiah 43:13).

God showed us the vision at its victory. Now we have to begin the adventure to get to the victorious outcome. Plan, be expecting to rise and build, increase and multiply. God will increase those who are called by His name, God called you. God chose you. We accept His invitation; our next step is to position ourselves to submit to God's order. Whatever we are building on right now, that investment is preparing us for a harvest. Everything God is getting us ready for is worth the wait; trust the transition process. Focus on God. Let Him transform us into the people He created us to be. We have to start appreciating the time we have right now, the things we have, and the people around us. Next year will be different; time will fly so quickly. Remember to stop, rest, reflect, and thank God. Pray every single day! Read the Bible every day to receive a word that will sustain and equip you. Every day is either a battle or a reward. God's presence needs to be in every area of our life, both the blessings and the pressure. All of that works together for our good.

Acts 16:14 (NIV)

One of those listening was a woman from the city of Thyatira named Lydia, a dealer in purple cloth. She was a worshiper of God. The Lord opened her heart to respond to Paul's message.

God opened Lydia's heart to receive the Word of God. God is opening your heart to receive His Word for salvation, repentance, and revival in your life, in your home, on your job, and everywhere you step your foot. The renewal of your heart is for you to share the good news of what Jesus has done for you. Revival restores your fellowship with God. How do we revive our relationship with God? We talk to God through prayer, singing, and speaking in the Spirit through our heavenly prayer language, through His Word. We revive our relationship with God when we follow His instructions. When He gives us a task, much is required of that task, especially the reliance on God Himself to accomplish the impossible. We build trust and fellowship through obedience. As we give and serve for the Kingdom of God, these are acts of our worship. As we worship, we give thanks and praise that draws in His presence. We study the scriptures to know God more. We study the scriptures so God can reveal Himself through the Word and give us clues toward our assignments and our call to a purpose that God fashioned for us individually and corporately. We align ourselves with the order and principles of the Kingdom of God.

Philippians 1:12-14 (AMP) The Gospel Is Preached

Now I want you to know, believers, that what has happened to me [this imprisonment that was meant to stop me] has actually served to advance [the spread of] the good news [regarding salvation]. My imprisonment in [the cause of] Christ has become common knowledge throughout the whole praetorian (imperial) guard and to everyone else. Because of my chains [seeing that I am doing well and that God is accomplishing great things], most of the brothers have renewed confidence in the Lord, and have far more courage to speak the word of God [concerning salvation] without fear [of the consequences, seeing that God can work His good in all circumstances].

God is always speaking and always moving. Remember we have a purpose and God wants us to keep moving forward. God's great plan for us is to go and share the good news of the Gospel of Christ in every area of our life. God wants us to multiply and prosper. In the darkest of nights, we are the star that shines the brightest. Be not ashamed of the Gospel of Christ; we are the key to salvation for those around us (Romans 1:16). The Kingdom of God's desire is about souls; save a soul with your testimony of how Jesus saved you. The army host of angels will rejoice with you as each soul is saved in your family. When they see the miracles God has done in our lives, they will wonder how do our lives look so blessed? Our response will always boast and praise the Lord. We are a master of faith to keep growing from faith to faith. We chose a life of integrity and a master of our destiny. In every circumstance, we are overcomers because our confidence is in the victory in Jesus.

2 Corinthians 9:10-11

Now he who supplies seed to the sower and bread for food will also supply and increase your store of seed and will enlarge the harvest of your righteousness.

You will be enriched in every way so that you can be generous on every occasion, and through us your generosity will result in thanksgiving to God.

We sow by planting seeds of the Word of God into those around us. We plant seeds of our finances into the ministry. We keep sowing into the dreams and visions standing on the Word of God through our hope, believing God will come through. We reap a harvest of blessings, gathering slowly, then the blessings gradually speed up. Then, we will end up sowing and reaping at the same time. Following that, the blessings will spread up, then the harvest is going to overtake us so that we will not have enough room to receive. We are going to have to start giving things away. Keep sowing then the harvest will overflow to our children and their children, then the blessings become generational blessings. When we plant seeds, we understand it takes time. Keep sowing into God. Sow in faith, sow in finances, sow in tears, sow in prayer, sow in obedience, sow in sacrifice, and sow in praise. Then, at the proper time, we'll see the blessing spout up. We do it again until we have a field of dreams and visions to accomplish that which keeps multiplying in good fruit, with a good harvest in good soil. We give others our fruit so they can start sowing their own seeds and grow their own harvest. You will multiply, you will have influence, and you will be a blessing even if you don't feel like anything is happening. Others are watching, seeing, and wondering at all the miracles that are happening around you and for you. Then, they realize it is God. God gave you favor because you were obedient, and you diligently sought Him in all things. DO NOT QUIT. Keep sowing, you are reaping good fruit with deep strong roots that will last for generations. God will give us a double reward for anything we missed when we stay planted in Him. We declare the Kingdom come and God's will be done on earth as it is in heaven.

Jeremiah 33:14-16

"'The days are coming,' declares the Lord, 'when I will fulfill the good promise I made to the people of Israel and Judah.

"'In those days and at that time
I will make a righteous Branch sprout from David's line;
he will do what is just and right in the land.
In those days Judah will be saved
and Jerusalem will live in safety.
This is the name by which it will be called:
The Lord Our Righteous Savior.'"

Jesus came to earth "to destroy the works of the devil" (1 John 2:7). The word "works" in this verse means the kind of energy that produces power or action. Jesus came to strip the devil of his power. The only power the enemy has over you is what you allow him to have through believing his lies. Every Christian has a calling. There is a general call, of course, to believe in Jesus Christ. But everyone who believes in Christ also has a special calling to a particular sphere of obedience, influence, and ministry. Jeremiah was not just set apart for salvation in a season that was ugly in the Old Testament, he was set apart for vocation. God had work for him to do. The young prophet had a mission to accomplish and a message to deliver to his generation. Remember some seasons are hard and can be extremely ugly. God allows for ugly seasons to happen for our good. God will allow the persecution and rejection for redirection in our lives. Restoration cannot happen without confrontation and unusual opposition. I know people say, "I go where I am celebrated and not tolerated." When we do things God's way, we break the order of the devil. We are out of sync with everyone else who operates in the flesh. The devil will use someone around us to tell us we are doing too much, they do not like what we are doing. We're trying to be something we are not. No, we are someone God called, and the enemy does not like that, the devil cannot control what God started. We are children of God; we have the mind and heart of Christ. We are covered by the blood to break the chains. We are doing what we are supposed to be doing. Anything the enemy says, immediately we go to God (NOT gossip to people) and say to God, "Show me Your truth of who I am in You." God always proves the enemy wrong, either in public or in private for our reassurance to move forward in Him. We do not need validation from people. Our validation comes from the Lord. This is not about worldly notoriety; it is about the Kingdom of God. The enemy knows our potential before we notice that God qualified us. This is not always an outward thing; a lot of our growth is private, too. There are times when God will not let us go where we are celebrated because He is using us in situations to uproot issues that have been tolerated before we came on the scene. God will restore and deliver in the ugly seasons. Always in a time of crisis, God uses the underdog to shift things despite adversity. In a time of crisis, there is a word to keep us and sustain us through the testing and hard times. God gave us a divine mission to accomplish, the enemy sees the power and the glory that is on us. That is why we were the target of the enemy's fiery darts. Even when we do not get the restitution we hoped for, we are still able to hug our enemies with mercy and say "Thank you" with sincere, gracious forgiveness. If it was not for the pressure, we would have never discovered who we are. It was good we were afflicted because we were learning, and God blessed us anyway. When we got overwhelmed, we got on our knees, submitted the weight to God and spoke His Word, spoke His promises, and spoke His praises over all that was happening. As all the craziness was going on, we were strengthened to keep pressing forward.

Proverbs 2:5-6

Then you will understand the fear of the Lord, and find the knowledge of God. For the Lord gives wisdom; out of His mouth come knowledge and understanding.

Our history gives hints to our destiny. Everything we have been through matters; it will be used by God. As you read the Bible more, the people and books that you gravitate more towards have a key paradigm to develop your purpose in Christ. Your relationship with God is not about traditional religious rituals. **Your relationship with God is a loving partnership through faith, love, and trust in your day-to-day actions.** God created you to be a worshiper unto Him. If you step into faith, God will provide all your needs. To walk this journey toward our destiny we have to know God, who He is, and what He does. The more we are knowledgeable in the Word of God, the stronger our journey. We have to build deep roots in the Word of God. Knowledge of God will increase and deepen the feeling of reverence toward Him. God is the only true fountain of wisdom. To receive that wisdom is to study the Word and apply the Word to your life and ask Him to impart the gift of wisdom unto you. It is only by the Holy Spirit that our zeal to live a life full of righteousness and self-control can be accomplished.

Proverbs 4:13 (NIV)

Hold on to instruction, do not let it go.
guard it well, for it is your life.

I heard it said the hardest part about walking in God's will, fulfilling the vision He gave you, is trying to understand if God is giving you signs to stop or is He testing our faith to keep going. Some people ask and cry for help and never receive the help they need from people. God is our help in times of trouble. God will never turn His back on you. He is our strength and refuge. When we get tired, we learn to rest and not quit. When we are stuck, we stop to give God praise and worship while we are in that waiting season until God instructs us for the next move. Keep walking with God and He will take care of you. Do not let bitterness overtake you, forgive and move on. Remember to smile. Although it cost all of you to change for the good, you're not alone on this journey. The change happens in your mind. Your perspective must be set on the Kingdom's goal, then everything else will fall into place. The more you change your mind, the more the sin and disorder will diminish. You have to see through a natural and supernatural vision and be open to correction. Let God guide your way now and eternally, submitting to His plan and not our agenda. Don't let people or roadblocks stop you. You have faith, not fear. Call on His great name and He will answer you. Thank God and praise His name every chance you get, especially when it gets rough. God gave you the victory, keep going, God will finish the good work He started in you. You got this!

2 Peter 1:5-8 (NIV)

For this very reason, make every effort to add to your faith goodness; and to goodness, knowledge; and to knowledge, self-control; and to self-control, perseverance; and to perseverance, godliness; and to godliness, mutual affection; and to mutual affection, love. For if you possess these qualities in increasing measure, they will keep you from being ineffective and unproductive in your knowledge of our Lord Jesus Christ.

ABOUT THE AUTHOR

Jamie Jeanette Barrera was born and raised in San Francisco California. Growing up in the Excelsior District, Jamie had faced opposition at a young age. Living in a broken home Jamie was surrounded by poverty, domestic violence, substance abuse, and life on the streets. God intervened when Jamie accepted Jesus as her Lord and Savior at age 17. However, with no firm foundation or support at the life-changing event of the passing of her grandmother and the calling off her engagement shortly after 9/11, Jamie was led into a downward spiral. It was during a wrong turn of working in nightclubs as a dancer and model where Jamie was scouted for well-known provocative men's magazines. It was during that time when Jamie had come to a crossroads during a camping trip to surrender her full life to Christ once more at age 25. With the birth of her daughter, Jamie took the steps toward overcoming her past having a new trust and firm foundation in Jesus. Through single motherhood and deep study of theology, Jamie became a student at Valor Christian College studying the office of Evangelism in Columbus, Ohio. Jamie accepted the call to ministry where she made it her mission to save souls for Jesus all across the country and worldwide. Jamie is also a "God's Leading Lady" alumnus through the Women to Women's ministry at The Potter's House in Dallas, Texas.

Jamie currently is highly involved in street ministry, trained by world-renowned Evangelist Debra George. Jamie travels to outreaches in communities of high gang violence, drugs, homelessness, and prostitution to win the lost to Christ in tough areas that are usually overlooked by society. Jamie also brings the love of Jesus back into nightclubs to minister to strippers and go-go dancers to help them out of the industry. Jamie is dedicated to her church outreach, spreading the light of salvation in the San Francisco Bay Area. Jamie helps lead "Socks for Souls" bringing socks and toiletries to the inner city of San Francisco's homeless community. Jamie speaks and mentors young girls, teens, and adults about choosing Jesus at the transition point from being a teen to adulthood with the practical application of the Gospel within their lives. She desires to see revival in big cities, especially San Francisco, like the ones of God's generals of the past with healings, signs, wonders, and miracles.

You will find Jamie with her daughter Celina enjoying being Disney super fans and making up silly songs. Along with traveling to win souls, they enjoy the local foodie treasures in every place they go. Jamie loves to read, salsa dancing, and singing Broadway showtunes in the car. If there is a game of trivia, Jamie and her daughter are up for the challenge.

REFERENCES

Bible Commentary:

© 2004 - 2020 by Bible Hub | https://Biblehub.com/

© 2001-2020, StudyLight.org | https://www.studylight.org/

© 2020 Blue Letter Bible | https://www.blueletterBible.org/

Walvoord, J. F. ed., & Zuck, R. B. ed. (1985). *The Bible Knowledge Commentary Old and New Testament.* Wheaton, IL: Victor Books.

Study Bibles:

© 2020 Bible Gateway | https://www.Biblegateway.com/

Green, J. P. (2014). *The Interlinear Hebrew-Greek-English Bible.* Peabody, MA: Hendrickson Publishers.

Keener, C. S., & Walton, J. H. (2016). *NIV Cultural Backgrounds Study Bible: Bringing to Life the Ancient World of Scripture.* Grand Rapids: Zondervan.

Spangler, A., & Neff, L. V. (2011). *The Names of God Bible.* Grand Rapids, MI: Revell.

Youngblood, R. F. (2014). *Nelson's Illustrated Bible Dictionary.* Harper Collins Christian Pub.

Books:

Bismark, T. (2011). *The Order of the Kingdom.* United States: Xulon Press.

Bismark, T. (n.d.). *Ministry in the House.* Sozo Publishing Group.

Bonhoeffer, D. (1972). *The Cost of Discipleship: Revised Edition Containing Material not Previously Translated.* New York: Macmillan.

Bounds, E. M. (2006). *E.M. Bounds on Prayer.* Peabody, MA: Hendrickson Christian Classics.

Coleman, R. E., & Graham, B. (2008). *The Master Plan of Evangelism.* Grand Rapids, MI: Revell.

Duncan-Williams, N. (n.d.). *Enforcing Prophetic Decrees Vol. 2 | Prayer Watch for Community Transformation.* Prayer Summit Publishing.

Eckhardt, J. (2015). *Prophet, Arise!* Lake Mary, FL: Charisma House.

Foster, R. J. (2018). *Celebration of Discipline: The Path to Spiritual Growth.* San Francisco: HarperOne.

Hayes, N. (1979). *From Heaven Come God's Weapons for the Church.* Tulsa: Harrison House.

Jakes, T. D. (2008). *Anointing Fall on Me: Accessing the Power of the Holy Spirit.* Shippensburg, PA: Destiny Image Publishers.

Munroe, M. (2018). *The Spirit of Leadership: Cultivating the Attitudes that Influence Human Action.* New Kensington, PA: Whitaker House.

Parsley, R. (2001). *Touched by the Anointing.* Columbus, OH: Results Pub.

Prince, D. (1998). *They Shall Expel Demons: What You Need to Know about Demons - Your Invisible Enemies.* S.l.: Baker Book House.

Spurgeon, C. H. (1963). *The Soul Winner: Or How to Lead Sinners to the Savior.* Grand Rapids, MI: Wm. B. Eerdmans Publishing Company.

Spurgeon, C. H. (1971). *Lectures to My Students.* Grand Rapids, MI: Associated Publishers and Authors.

Stone, P. (2011). *How to Interpret Dreams and Visions. Understanding God's Warnings and Guidance.* OCI Ministries.

Sumrall, L. (1982). *The Gifts and Ministries of the Holy Spirit.* New Kensington, PA : Whitaker House.

Swaggart, J. (2016). *Elisha.* Baton Rouge, LA: Jimmy Swaggart Ministries

Tozer, A. W. (1996). *The Knowledge of the Holy: The Attributes of God: Their Meaning in the Christian Life.* New York: Walker.

Tozer, A. W. (2014). *Voice of the Prophet, Who speaks for God?*

Now that you have read, I'm Saved! Now What? I would really appreciate it if you could please post a review on Amazon. I look forward to reading about how reading this book has blessed you.

Thank you.

Jamie Barrera AKA The Tiny Princess

INDEX

A

B

C

D

E

F

G

H

K

L

M

N

R

S

T

Please post a review at
HigginsPublishing.com or at Amazon
to let Jamie, know that you enjoyed this book.

Sign up for Jamie's newsletter for giveaways, encouragement and free content at JamieJBarrera.com.

~~~

Request prayer, volunteer for outreach, donate, or schedule Jamie for speaking engagements and virtual tours at, JamieJBarrera.com.

Please share Jamie's posts and podcasts at her website to help others with their Christian journey.

Thank you!

A percentage of the proceeds from sales of "I'm Saved! Now What?" are donated to Jamie's non-profit organization at JamieJBarrera.com.

I'm Saved! Now What?
Is also available in the following formats:
Audiobook & Ebook in English,
Paperback & Ebook in Spanish.
~~~

Made in United States
Orlando, FL
11 May 2023

33056066R00154